The Economics of Natural and Unnatural Disasters

The Economics of Natural and Unnatural Disasters

William Kern
Editor

2010

THE PAPERS IN THIS VOLUME WERE
PRESENTED AT THE 2008-2009
WERNER SICHEL LECTURE-SEMINAR
SERIES HELD AT WESTERN
MICHIGAN UNIVERSITY.

W.E. Upjohn Institute for Employment Research
Kalamazoo, Michigan

Library of Congress Cataloging-in-Publication Data

The economics of natural and unnatural disasters / William Kern, editor.
  p. cm.
  Includes bibliographical references and index.
  ISBN-13: 978-0-88099-362-3 (pbk. : alk. paper)
  ISBN-10: 0-88099-362-6 (pbk. : alk. paper)
  ISBN-13: 978-0-88099-363-0 (hbk. : alk. paper)
  ISBN-10: 0-88099-363-4 (hbk. : alk. paper)
  1. Disasters—economic aspects. I. Kern, William S., 1952– II. W.E. Upjohn
Institute for Employment Research.
  HC79.D45E25 2010
  363.34—dc22
                                        2010010590

Cover design by Alcorn Publication Design.
Index prepared by Diane Worden.
Printed in the United States of America.
Printed on recycled paper.

Contents

1
Introduction

William Kern
Western Michigan University

Throughout history mankind has been subject to disasters produced by "Mother Nature" as well as the man-made variety. Only recently, however, have economists understood disasters as economic phenomena to be formally analyzed. Given the magnitude of many recent disasters, their impact on local, regional, and national economies, and the coverage of their consequences in the popular press, it is puzzling that the attention of economists was for so long largely diverted from analysis of these events. Perhaps George Stigler has already provided the answer to this puzzle in his Nobel lecture, where he observed that economists have frequently neglected the study of important current events. He points out, for example, that "during the Industrial Revolution, economists adopted the law of diminishing returns but ignored the most widespread growth of output that the world had yet observed." The explanation that he offered, perhaps tongue in cheek, was that "the scholars who create economic theory do not read the newspapers regularly or carefully during working hours" (1992, p. 61).

We are now observing, happily, a reversal of this practice, as more economists have begun to study the economics of disasters during the past several decades. Although the number of economists who study disasters is still small, the economics of disasters appears to be well on the road to establishing itself as an important subdiscipline in economics.

Why are economists now more likely to pay attention to disasters? As Howard C. Kunreuther and Erwann O. Michel-Kerjan report in their chapter, "Market and Government Failure in Insuring and Mitigating Natural Catastrophes: How Long-Term Contracts Can Help," disasters were, for much of history, regarded as low-probability events. However, they argue that we are now entering "a new era of catastrophes" in which disasters occur with greater frequency and the losses are of a much greater magnitude than in the past. Why are disasters occurring more frequently and why are the losses increasing? Kunreuther and Michel-Kerjan offer several reasons for the greater magnitude and greater frequency of disasters. One prominent change in recent decades is a significant increase in the population concentrated in urban areas on coasts, which puts more people at risk of losses due to hurricanes and tsunamis. The greater level of economic development in coastal areas has also increased the magnitude of losses. Kunreuther and Michel-Kerjan suggest that global climate change may be at work as well. They point out that of the 20 biggest catastrophes occurring between 1970 and 2004, more than 80 percent were weather-related.

Kunreuther and Michel-Kerjan therefore suggest that the time has come to develop a better strategy for coping with disasters. In their opinion, the recent losses suffered in these catastrophic events suggest that inadequate preparation and inadequate mitigation efforts have been the norm. This, they argue, is due in large part to myopia and misperception of the actual risks, both by potential victims and policymakers.

What do they suggest should be done? Kunreuther and Michel-Kerjan offer several guiding principles designed to stimulate greater mitigation efforts and minimize insurance losses while still offering protection against catastrophe. The primary guiding principle is that insurance should be priced in accordance with risk. They argue that such pricing will create incentives to invest in mitigation efforts, citing substantial evidence for the significant benefits of mitigation. Unfortunately, typical property owners will be unlikely to bear the high up-front cost of mitigation efforts in light of the uncertainty of short-run cost savings. Kunreuther and Michel-Kerjan therefore argue for the development of long-term insurance contracts designed to induce property owners to take a long-run view of the problem. However, they recognize that forces on both the supply side and the demand side militate against the emergence of markets for this type of insurance contract. They therefore suggest government action to help create such markets. They argue that the National Flood Insurance Program might offer the best opportunity to create long-term insurance markets and demonstrate the usefulness of long-term insurance policies and thus encourage their development.

While Kunreuther and Michel-Kerjan are able to demonstrate the potential benefits of long-term insurance arrangements, doubt remains regarding the political will to undertake what is necessary to make them viable. As they point out, private long-term insurance contracts have failed to emerge in part because of government policy. State government insurance regulators have, unfortunately, largely resisted efforts by insurance companies to raise premiums to reflect risks. In fact, there is increasing pressure on state insurance regulators in high-risk states such as Florida to *reduce* insurance rates rather than increase them. The general public often believes that insurance companies have made enormous profits at their expense and that current insurance rates are unnecessarily high due to the greed of insurance executives. It will be a hard sell to convince the public, as well as politicians, who depend on public support, of the necessity of raising rates to reflect risks. While pricing insurance to reflect risks is good economics, such a strategy would entail a high likelihood of loss for politicians who support it.

Anthony M. Yezer's chapter, "Expectations and Unexpected Consequences of Public Policy toward Natural and Man-Made Disasters," focuses on the significance of changes in the expectations of disasters for our understanding of their economic impact. He points out that the infrequency of disasters, the spatial concentration of their effects, and the size of disasters all raise the possibility that the expectations of disasters will change as a consequence of their occurrence. He cites this as a distinguishing feature of disasters in comparison with hazards generally considered. In fact, he claims that this is the most underresearched aspect of the economics of disasters.

Yezer's analysis of the impact of disasters on disaster expectations reveals several possible models of response. His analysis is based on the assumption that disaster expectations are formed on the basis of a comparison of recent disaster occurrences with the historical record. An increase in the frequency of disasters thus raises the expectations of disasters. From this model of disaster expectation he draws conclusions about the relations between economic growth and disasters, the incentives to develop land in disaster-prone areas, and the significance of disaster expectations for insurance markets and public policy toward disasters. Several puzzles regarding the relations between disasters and economic growth, the optimal development of land in hazardous areas, and the market for disaster insurance can be better understood once one considers that the occurrence of disasters will also change the expectations of disasters.

One of the important lessons he derives from his analysis is the need to distinguish between expected and unexpected disasters in considering the economic impact of disasters. The magnitude of the economic losses a disaster produces depends crucially on the difference between expected losses and unanticipated losses. Among the conclusions Yezer derives from this analysis is that the economic effects of a disaster are dependent not only on the physical severity of the event but also on the extent to which the event and its damage were anticipated. He therefore concludes that government aid to disaster areas should be concentrated on unanticipated disasters. While he recognizes that politically this may not be feasible, he does find evidence that several federal disaster relief policies adhere in some respects to this principle.

Hal Cochrane's chapter, "The Economics of Disaster: Retrospect and Prospect," provides an overview of the development of the economics of disasters. Its insights into reasons underlying the development of the field will be of particular value to readers new to this subject. Cochrane demonstrates that the analysis of disaster mitigation efforts was developed largely as an application of water resource economics combined with insights from the economics of information. He provides an excellent survey of the nature of the cost-loss trade-offs involved in managing hazards as well as a very useful discussion of the value of disaster forecasts in this framework. His application of this model to the case of rising CO_2 emissions and the uncertainty of the forecasts of global warming is a simple but powerful example of the insights that can be derived from the cost-loss model.

Cochrane points out that a correct estimate of losses is a key element in the cost-loss framework. In contrast to Yezer, Cochrane holds the opinion that the housing markets provide little good evidence about the extent to which hazards and particularly disasters are capitalized in housing and land values. As a result he concludes that analysis of housing and land market values offers an inadequate measure of the willingness to pay for safety. He also points out that disasters yield several distinct sorts of losses that are contentious and difficult to measure, including the loss of cultural community and assets of a historical nature.

The chapter concludes with a discussion about the use of input-output analysis as a means of measuring the impact of disasters on local and regional economies. In Cochrane's opinion, input-output analysis, while a useful tool in the right context, has a fatal flaw in its application to disasters, in that it is incapable of addressing the impacts of the supply-side bottlenecks in local and regional economies that occur in the aftermath of disasters. Input-output analysis does not account for insufficient capacity. It is driven by variations on the demand side and thus is inadequate to analyze the supply-side shocks so common in disaster situations. Other techniques such as computable general equilibrium models and econometric analysis are also found wanting in important respects. Cochrane concludes with the advice that the unique nature of these events implies that it might be difficult to draw general lessons about the impact of disasters and to predict the pace of recovery, when such analysis is often based on factors present in the predisaster setting but absent in the postdisaster environment.

While much of the literature in the economics of disasters focuses on market failures and the role of government in postdisaster relief efforts, Peter Boettke and Daniel Smith, in their chapter, "Private Solutions to Public Disasters: Self-Reliance and Social Resilience," examine the much-neglected role of the private sector and markets in the postdisaster recovery process, using post-Katrina New Orleans as an example. They point out that while most of the discussion is focused on the role that government should play, one needs to consider the important role that private entities—both for-profit and nonprofit—can and do play in the recovery process. Furthermore, they argue that one should also consider that the attempts by private entities to cope with the recovery process are often thwarted by government actions both pre- and postdisaster. For example, in New Orleans, government policies encouraged people to locate in flood-prone areas and left them vulnerable to loss because of inadequately constructed levees. In the aftermath of Katrina, occupational and building code regulations thwarted private recovery efforts and distorted the set of price signals necessary to ensure efficient use of the available resources.

Boettke and Smith argue that the price system and private efforts must be and have been an integral part of disaster recovery. However, in disaster situations we are likely to want to suspend the use of the market and distort the price signals necessary to help with the recovery process, perhaps out of public concern to keep someone from profiting at the expense of others. But Boettke and Smith argue that the pursuit by entrepreneurs of profitable opportunities created by the disaster is the basis of the economic recovery and that efforts to thwart those pursuits are misguided and delay the recovery. Ironically, for-profit entities often were the most civic-minded, responsive, and generous to the community in the aftermath of Katrina.

Daniel Sutter and Kevin M. Simmons, in their chapter, "The Socioeconomic Impact of Tornadoes," point out that tornadoes constitute one of the most common and frequent forms of disaster; they occur in all 50 states and throughout the year. The authors concentrate on three issues: the trend of losses due to tornadoes, the role of the National Weather Service's tornado warning program, and the cost-effectiveness of several tornado loss-mitigation strategies. Their research yields some surprising results. They estimate that the largest segment of losses caused by tornadoes—approximately two-thirds of the total—is the opportunity cost of time spent under tornado warnings. That so much of the cost can be attributed to time spent under warnings is partly accounted for by the steady decrease in the losses attributable to tornado fatalities during the past half-century.

The paper devotes considerable discussion to the factors contributing to tornado losses, including the time of day, the severity of the winds, the location of the storm, and even the day of the week. However, of greatest interest to economists will be the authors' discussion of potential ways to minimize tornado losses and their estimates of the cost-effectiveness of several mitigation strategies. Sutter and Simmons find that attempts to minimize the time spent under warning have the greatest potential, given that this time is the largest component of costs. They claim that the recently adopted use of Storm-Based Warnings by the National Weather Service has the potential to reduce losses by as much as $1 billion per year. In addition, increasing the lead time of warnings also appears to be a cost-effective strategy, up to a point.

Conversely, Sutter and Simmons find that tornado shelters are rarely cost-effective means of reducing casualty losses, in that the cost to save a life exceeds the value statistically assigned to a life. They estimate that even with the widespread use of shelters in a tornado-prone area like Oklahoma, it would cost about $57 million per life saved. However, they do find that significant value has resulted from the more stringent regulation of manufactured home construction mandated by HUD in 1994. They find that these regulations have reduced losses stemming from casualties significantly and in a relatively cost-effective manner, especially when compared to the cost of building shelters.

The chapters presented here give the reader a sample of the sort of research now being undertaken on the economics of disasters. Several themes long dominant in this literature are thoroughly discussed. These include the ability of potential disaster victims to accurately assess the risks they face, the role of incentives in ensuring that mitigation efforts are undertaken, the adequacy of our evaluation of the impact of disasters on economies, and discussion of the effectiveness of current government policies toward disaster prevention and relief. These will in all likelihood continue to be topics of discussion in the future as well. I hope the following chapters will give readers insight into the current state of debate on these issues.

Reference

Stigler, George. 1992. "The Process and Progress of Economics." In *Lectures, Economics 1981–1990*, Karl-Göran Mäler, ed. Singapore: World Scientific Publishing Co., pp. 57–76. http://nobelprize.org/nobel_prizes/economics/laureates/1982/stigler-lecture.pdf (accessed October 27, 2009).

2
Market and Government Failure in Insuring and Mitigating Natural Catastrophes

How Long-Term Contracts Can Help

Howard C. Kunreuther
Erwann O. Michel-Kerjan
University of Pennsylvania

Insurance plays a vital role in America's economy by helping households and businesses manage risks . . . When insurance prices reflect underlying economic costs they can encourage a more efficient allocation of resources. Efforts to keep premiums for insurance against catastrophe hazards artificially low, whether through regulation or through subsidized government programs, can encourage excessively risky behavior on the part of those who might be affected by future catastrophes.

—Council of Economic Advisers (2007)[1]

Given the hundreds of billions of dollars in economic losses due to catastrophes in the United States since 2001, it is difficult to realize that when Hurricane Hugo hit the country in 1989, it was the first catastrophe to inflict more than $1 billion in insured losses. But times have changed because of a series of unprecedented large-scale natural disasters in the United States during the past few years. Times have changed because of the increased terrorism threat worldwide, including the potential for nuclear attacks. Times have changed because of the possibility of international pandemics and world cyber-failure, and because of the financial crises we are currently experiencing. In other words, we have entered a new era of catastrophes.

While all of the above risks are different in character, they share two important features: 1) uncertainty regarding their occurrence and 2) wide variance in losses from one year to the next. Experts and decision makers face challenges in assessing the risks associated with these extreme events, in developing strategies for reducing future losses, and in facilitating the recovery process following a major catastrophe.

As for natural disasters, the world has experienced large-scale losses and fatalities because of the increasing concentration of population and activities in high-risk coastal regions. In Southeast Asia, the tsunami in December 2004 killed more than 280,000 people residing in coastal areas. Cyclone Nargis, which made landfall in Myanmar in May 2008, killed an estimated 140,000 people, making it the deadliest natural disaster in the country's recorded history. The same month, the Great Sichuan Earthquake in China is estimated to have killed nearly 70,000 people, injured 374,000, and made almost 5 million homeless (Munich Re 2008). Deaths from the Haitian earthquake in January 2010 are estimated at 200,000 (European Commission 2010).

But even in a developed country like the United States, which has both extensive experience with natural catastrophes and the resources to adequately prepare for them, the 2004 and 2005 hurricane seasons demonstrated a lack of adequate loss reduction measures and emergency preparedness capacity to deal with large-scale natural disasters. Hurricane Katrina, which hit Louisiana and Mississippi at the end of August 2005, killed 1,300 people and forced 1.5 million people to evacuate the affected area—a record number for the country. Economic damages were estimated in the range of $150 billion to $200 billion.

After two relatively quiet hurricane seasons in 2006 and 2007 in the United States, a series of hurricanes made landfall in 2008, causing billions of dollars in direct economic losses along the Caribbean Basin and in the United States. Hurricane Ike was the most expensive individual event in 2008, with an estimated privately insured loss of $16 billion, followed by Hurricane Gustav, with insured losses estimated at $4 billion. Based on these figures, Hurricane Ike ranks as the third most devastating weather-related disaster in U.S. history, after Hurricane Katrina and Hurricane Andrew, which hit southeast Florida in August 1992 (Swiss Re 2008).

These recent catastrophes highlight the challenges of mitigating the effects of natural disasters and financing recovery from them, issues that are now high on the business and policy agendas of many countries. The question is not whether other large-scale catastrophes will occur, but when and how frequently they will strike, and the extent of the damage and fatalities they will cause. Now is the time to develop and implement economically sound policies and strategies for managing the risk and consequences of future disasters. It is important for us to take a longer-term view of these issues, given the tendency of individuals to be myopic in their thinking and to misperceive risks. A coherent strategy is necessary to ensure a sustainable recovery from large-scale disasters and the appropriate future development of hazard-prone areas. But these issues are complex. They challenge our capacity as a nation to work together despite different agendas of key stakeholders and legislators regarding the role and responsibilities of the private and public sectors in dealing with catastrophic risks. Absence of leadership in this area will inevitably lead to unnecessary loss of lives and economic destruction in the devastated regions.

This chapter complements other analyses in this volume by focusing on the risk of large-scale natural disasters, although we believe the concepts and proposals for managing these risks more effectively have relevance to other types of extreme events such as terrorism and catastrophic accidents.[2] The chapter is organized as follows: in the next section we discuss the evolution over the past four decades of economic and insured losses due to major catastrophes and the key drivers of this change. We then propose four guiding principles for developing sustainable insurance and mitigation programs and analyze the behavioral biases, notably myopia, that discourage individuals from investing in cost-effective protective measures. To overcome these biases, we propose long-term insurance contracts combined with long-term loans. We then demonstrate how the National Flood Insurance Program is a natural candidate for these contracts. The chapter concludes with a brief summary and suggestions for future research.

A NEW ERA OF CATASTROPHES

Recent Changes in the Impacts of Extreme Events

The economic and insured losses from great natural catastrophes such as hurricanes, earthquakes, and floods worldwide have increased significantly in recent years, as shown in Figure 2.1. (Each vertical bar represents the total economic losses, and the darker zone represents the insured portion of it.) A comparison of these economic losses over time reveals a huge increase: $53.6 billion (1950–1959), $93.3 billion (1960–1969), $161.7 billion (1970–1979), $262.9 billion (1980–1989), and $778.3 billion (1990–1999). Between 2000 and 2008, losses totaled $620.6 billion, principally as a result of the 2004, 2005, and 2008 hurricane seasons, which wrought historic levels of destruction.

Figure 2.1 Evolution of Great Natural Catastrophes Worldwide, 1950–2008

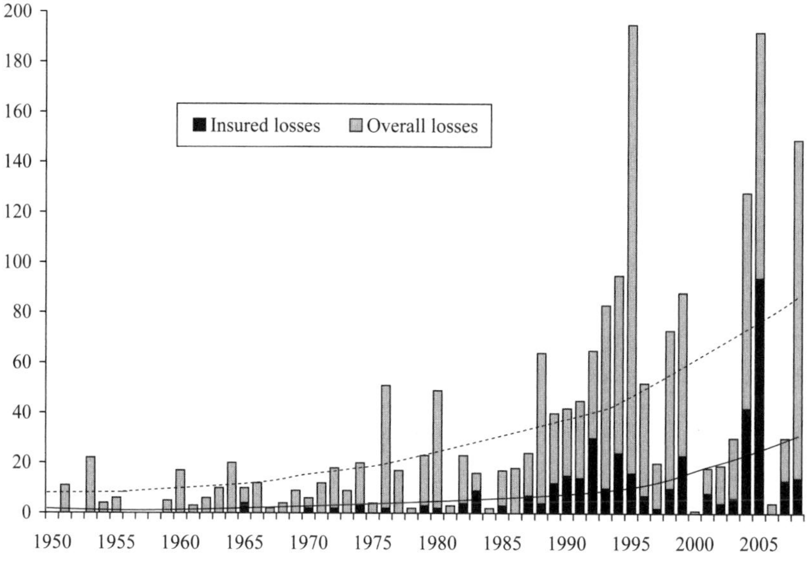

NOTE: In billions of U.S. dollars, indexed to 2008. Dotted line indicates trend in overall losses. Solid line indicates trend in insured losses.
SOURCE: Munich Re (2009a).

Catastrophes have had a more devastating impact on insurers since 1990 than in the entire history of insurance. Between 1970 and the mid-1980s, annual insured losses from natural disasters (including forest fires) were in the $3 billion to $4 billion range. The insured losses from Hurricane Hugo, which made landfall in Charleston, South Carolina, in September 1989, exceeded $4 billion (in 1989 dollars). There was a radical increase in insured losses in the early 1990s, as Hurricane Andrew struck Florida ($23.7 billion in 2007 dollars) and the Northridge earthquake hit California ($19.6 billion in 2007 dollars). The four hurricanes that struck Florida in 2004 (Charley, Frances, Ivan, and Jeanne) collectively totaled almost $33 billion in insured losses. Hurricane Katrina alone cost insurers and reinsurers an estimated $46 billion, and total losses paid by private insurers resulting from major natural catastrophes in 2005 reached $87 billion.[3] Figure 2.2 depicts the upward trend in worldwide insured losses from catastrophes between 1970 and 2008.[4]

Table 2.1 reveals the 25 most costly insured catastrophes from 1970 to 2008 (in 2008 dollars). Of these 25 major events, 14 occurred after 2001, and 12 of happened in the United States. Hurricane Andrew and the Northridge earthquake were the first two catastrophes that the industry experienced with losses greater than $10 billion (designated as super-cats), and they caused insurers to reflect on whether risks from natural disasters were still insurable. To assist them in making this determination, many firms began using catastrophe models to estimate the likelihood and consequences to their insured portfolios from specific disasters in hazard-prone areas (Grossi and Kunreuther 2005). With the exception of the terrorist attacks on September 11, 2001, all of the events in the top 25 were natural disasters. More than 80 percent of these were weather-related events—hurricanes and typhoons, storms, and floods—and nearly three-quarters of the claims were made in the United States.

Losses resulting from natural catastrophes and man-made disasters in 2006 were far below the losses in 2004 and 2005. Of the $48 billion in catastrophe-related economic losses, $16 billion was covered by insurance ($11 billion for natural disasters and $5 billion for man-made). During the past 25 years, only 1988 and 1997 had insured losses lower than those in 2006. According to Munich Re (2008), there were 960

Figure 2.2   Worldwide Evolution of Catastrophe-Insured Losses, 1970–2008

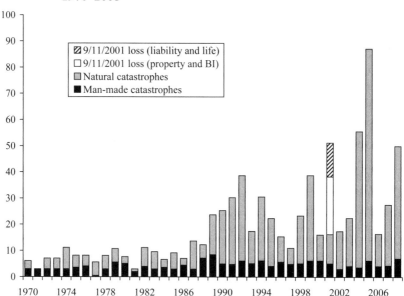

NOTE: Man-made catastrophes include major fires and explosions (e.g., in a chemical plant or refinery), aviation/rail/shipping-related losses (fires, crashes, collisions), mining accidents, and collapse of infrastructure. The bar for 2001, because it includes the terrorist attacks of 9/11, is broken down into two additional categories that represent all the various types of insurance, including not only liability and life but also property and business interruption (BI). Losses are shown in billions of U.S. dollars indexed for 2007, except for 2008, which is current.
SOURCE: Wharton Risk Center, with data from Swiss Re and the Insurance Information Institute.

natural catastrophes in 2007, the most since 1974. They inflicted nearly $27 billion in insured losses. Swiss Re estimates that insured losses soared to $50 billion for the industry in 2008, making it one of the three costliest years ever. Natural catastrophes accounted for $43 billion of these losses, with man-made disasters making up the remaining $7 billion (Swiss Re 2008). In 2009, insured losses from catastrophes amounted to $22 billion, a lower figure due to a very benign North Atlantic hurricane season (Munich Re 2009b).

The occurrence of damaging hurricanes is highly variable and uncertain from year to year. However, it is almost certain that in the coming years more catastrophic hurricanes will strike the Atlantic and Gulf coasts. Other parts of the nation will experience severe floods (as occurred in the Upper Midwest in 2008) and earthquakes, causing extreme damage to residential and commercial property and infrastructure.

There is a very clear message from these data. Only 20 or 30 years ago, large-scale natural disasters were considered low-probability events. Today, not only are they causing considerably greater economic losses than in the past, they also appear to be occurring at an accelerating pace. In this context, it is important to understand more fully the factors influencing these changes so as to design more effective programs for reducing losses from future disasters.

The Question of Attribution

At least two principal socioeconomic factors directly influence the level of economic losses due to catastrophic events: 1) degree of urbanization and 2) value at risk. In 1950, approximately 30 percent of the world's population lived in cities. In 2000, about 50 percent of the world's population (6 billion) resided in urban areas. Projections by the United Nations (2004) show that by 2025, that figure will have increased to 60 percent, based on a world population estimate of 8.3 billion people.

In the United States in 2003, 53 percent of the nation's population, or 153 million people, lived in the 673 U.S. coastal counties, an increase of 33 million people since 1980, according to the National Oceanic and Atmospheric Administration (NOAA). And the nation's coastal population is expected to increase by more than 12 million by 2015 (Crossett et al. 2004).[5] Yet coastal counties, excluding Alaska, account for only 17 percent of the land area in the United States.

In hazard-prone areas, this urbanization and increase of population also translates into greater concentration of exposure and hence a higher likelihood of catastrophic losses from future disasters. Insurance density is another critical socioeconomic factor to consider when evaluating the evolution of insured loss due to weather-related catastrophes. These factors will continue to have a major impact on the level of insured

Table 2.1 The 25 Most Costly Insured Catastrophes in the World, 1970–2008

Event	$ billions	Victims (dead or missing)	Year	Area of primary damage
Hurricane Katrina	48.1	1,836	2005	U.S., Gulf of Mexico, et al.
9/11 attacks	36.8	3,025	2001	U.S.
Hurricane Andrew	24.6	43	1992	U.S., Bahamas
Northridge earthquake	20.3	61	1994	U.S.
Hurricane Ike	17.6	348	2008	U.S., Caribbean, et al.
Hurricane Ivan	14.6	124	2004	U.S., Caribbean, et al.
Hurricane Wilma	13.8	35	2005	U.S., Gulf of Mexico, et al.
Hurricane Rita	11.1	34	2005	U.S., Gulf of Mexico, et al.
Hurricane Charley	9.1	24	2004	U.S., Caribbean, et al.
Typhoon Mireille	8.9	51	1991	Japan
Hurricane Hugo	7.9	71	1989	Puerto Rico, U.S., et al.
Winter Storm Daria	7.7	95	1990	France, UK, et al.
Winter Storm Lothar	7.5	110	1999	France, Switzerland, et al.
Winter Storm Kyrill	6.3	54	2007	Germany, UK, the Netherlands, France
Storms and floods	5.9	22	1987	France, UK, et al.

Hurricane Frances	5.8	38	2004	U.S., Bahamas
Winter Storm Vivian	5.2	64	1990	Western/Central Europe
Typhoon Bart	5.2	26	1999	Japan
Hurricane Gustav	5.0	153	2008	U.S., Caribbean, et al.
Hurricane Georges	4.7	600	1998	U.S., Caribbean
Tropical Storm Allison	4.4	41	2001	U.S.
Hurricane Jeanne	4.4	3,034	2004	U.S., Caribbean, et al.
Typhoon Songda	4.0	45	2004	Japan, South Korea
Storms	3.7	45	2003	U.S.
Hurricane Floyd	3.6	70	1999	U.S., Bahamas, Columbia

NOTE: Dollar amounts are indexed to 2008.
SOURCE: Kunreuther and Michel-Kerjan (2009), with data from Swiss Re (2009) and the Insurance Information Institute in New York.

losses from natural catastrophes. Given the growing concentration of exposure on the Gulf Coast, another hurricane like Katrina hitting that area is likely to inflict significant property damage unless strong mitigation measures are put in place.[6]

In order to better understand this new vulnerability, it is possible to calculate the total direct economic cost of the major hurricanes in the United States in the past century, adjusted for inflation, population, and wealth normalization. More specifically, one can estimate what each of these hurricanes would have cost had it hit today. This exercise has been done in several studies. The most recent one, by Pielke et al. (2008), normalizes to the year 2005 mainland U.S. hurricane damage for the period 1900–2005.

Table 2.2 provides estimates for the top 20 most costly hurricanes if they had occurred in 2005, using two approaches for normalizing these losses, each of which gives a cost estimate. The table indicates the range of costs provided by these two estimates, the year the hurricane occurred, the states that were most seriously affected, and the hurricane category on the Saffir-Simpson scale. The data reveal that the hurricane that hit Miami in 1926 would have been almost twice as costly as Hurricane Katrina had it occurred in 2005, and the Galveston hurricane of 1900 would have had total direct economic costs as high as those from Katrina. This means that independent of any possible change in weather patterns, we are very likely to see even more devastating disasters in the coming years because of the ongoing growth in value located in risk-prone areas.

There is another element to consider in determining how to adequately manage and finance catastrophic risks: the possible impact of a change in climate on future weather-related catastrophes. Between 1970 and 2004, storms and floods were responsible for over 90 percent of the total economic costs of extreme weather-related events worldwide. Storms (hurricanes in the U.S. region, typhoons in Asia, and windstorms in Europe) contributed to over 75 percent of insured losses. In constant prices (2004), insured losses from weather-related events averaged $3 billion annually between 1970 and 1990 and then increased significantly to $16 billion annually between 1990 and 2004 (Association of British Insurers 2005). In 2005, 99.7 percent of all catastrophic losses worldwide were due to weather-related events (Mills and Lecomte 2006).

Table 2.2 Top 20 Hurricane Scenarios, Ranked Using 2005 Inflation, Population, and Wealth Normalization (1900–2005)

Rank	Hurricane	Year	Category	Cost range ($ billion) in 2005
1	Miami (southeast FL/MS/AL)	1926	4	140–157
2	Katrina (LA/MS)	2005	3	81
3	North Texas (Galveston)	1900	4	72–78
4	North Texas (Galveston)	1915	4	57–62
5	Andrew (southeast FL and LA)	1992	5–3	54–60
6	New England (CT/MA/NY/RI)	1938	3	37–39
7	Southwest Florida	1944	3	35–39
8	Lake Okeechobee (southeast Florida)	1928	4	32–34
9	Donna (FL/NC/NY)	1960	4–3	29–32
10	Camille (MS/southeast LA/VA)	1969	5	21–24
11	Betsy (southeast FL and LA)	1965	3	21–23
12	Wilma	2005	3	21
13	Agnes (FL/CT/NY)	1972	1	17–18
14	Diane (NC)	1955	1	17
15	4 (southeast FL/LA/AL/MS)	1947	4–3	15–17
16	Hazel (SC/NC)	1954	4	16–23
17	Charley (southwest FL)	2004	4	16
18	Carol (CT/NY/RI)	1954	3	15–16
19	Hugo (SC)	1989	4	15–16
20	Ivan (northwest FL/AL)	2004	3	15

SOURCE: Data from Pielke et al. (2008).

Numerous discussions and scientific debates have centered on whether the series of major hurricanes in 2004 and 2005 might be partially attributable to the impact of a change in climate.[7] One of the expected effects of global warming is an increase in hurricane intensity. This has been predicted by theory and modeling, and substantiated by empirical data on climate change. Higher ocean temperatures lead to an exponentially higher evaporation rate in the atmosphere, which increases the intensity of cyclones and precipitation. The results to date raise issues with respect to the insurability of weather-related catastrophes, given that an increase in the number of major hurricanes over a shorter period of time is likely to translate into a greater number hitting the coasts, with a greater likelihood of damage to a much larger number of residences and commercial buildings today than in the 1940s.

The combination of increasing urbanization, concentration of value in high-risk areas, and the potential impact of a change in weather patterns raises questions as to how the insurance industry will provide protection against catastrophic risks in the future. Traditional insurance relies on geographical and time diversification, both of which are somewhat compromised by these recent trends. The appropriate adoption of roles and responsibilities by the private and public sectors (as a source of financial support or as a market regulator) is critical in this regard.

GUIDING PRINCIPLES FOR MITIGATING AND INSURING AGAINST CATASTROPHES

To help ascertain the roles the private and public sectors can play in addressing these issues, we propose the following four guiding principles for using the insurance infrastructure to deal more effectively with natural disasters:

Principle 1—Premiums should reflect risk. Insurance premiums should be based on risk in order to provide signals to individuals as to the hazards they face and to encourage them to engage in cost-effective mitigation measures to reduce their vulnerability to catastrophes. Risk-based premiums should also reflect the cost of capital that insurers need to integrate into their pricing to ensure adequate return to their investors. The application of Principle 1 provides a clear signal of likely damage to those currently residing in areas subject to natural disasters and those who are considering moving into these regions. Risk-based premiums would also enable insurers to provide discounts to homeowners and businesses that invest in cost-effective loss-reduction mitigation measures. If insurance premiums are not risk-based, insurers have no economic incentive to offer these discounts. In fact, they prefer not to offer coverage to these property owners because it is a losing proposition in the long run.

Principle 2—Deal with equity and affordability issues. Any special treatment given to homeowners currently residing in hazard-prone areas (e.g., low-income uninsured or inadequately insured homeowners) should come from general public funding and not through insurance premium subsidies.

Principle 2 reflects a concern for some residents in high-hazard areas who will be faced with large premium increases if insurers are permitted to adhere to Principle 1. As discussed in the next section, regulations imposed by state insurance commissioners keep premiums in many regions subject to hurricane damage artificially lower than the risk-based level.

Note that Principle 2 applies only to individuals who currently reside in a hazard-prone area. Those who decide to move to the area in the future should be charged premiums that reflect the risk. If they were provided with financial assistance from public sources to purchase insurance, the resulting public policy would directly encourage development in hazard-prone areas and exacerbate the potential for catastrophic losses from future disasters.

Principle 3—Have sufficient demand for coverage. The demand by individuals and firms for insurance coverage with risk-based premiums should be sufficiently high that insurers can cover the fixed costs of introducing a program for providing coverage and spreading the risk broadly throughout their portfolios. High demand for insurance would also reduce the level of state and federal relief to uninsured or underinsured homeowners in the aftermath of the next disaster.

Principle 4—Minimize likelihood of insolvency. Insurers and reinsurers should determine how much coverage to offer, and what premium to charge against the risk so that the chances of insolvency are below some predefined acceptable level.

Insurance regulators should play an important role in ensuring that insurers providing coverage in high-risk areas have a solid financial basis for doing so.

THE BEHAVIORAL CHALLENGES: THE DEMAND FOR INSURANCE AND MITIGATION

How effective can mitigation be in reducing exposure to future disaster? To shed some light on this question, we undertook an analysis of the impact that mitigation would have on reducing losses from hurricanes in four states: Florida, New York, South Carolina, and Texas (Kunreuther and Michel-Kerjan 2009). In our analysis we consider two extreme cases: one in which no one has invested in mitigation, and one in which everyone has invested in predefined mitigation measures. From the U.S. Hurricane Model developed by the catastrophe modeling firm Risk Management Solutions, losses were calculated on a ground-up and gross basis, assuming an appropriate mitigation measure across the insured portfolio. The mitigation measures were selected based on various assumptions for the different regions. For example, in Florida, the requirements were those defined by the Institute for Business and Home Safety's "Fortified . . . for safer living" program. As this program is only for new construction, when we describe an analysis using these recommendations, it is the retrofit techniques that are aligned with the features of the Fortified program. In New York, South Carolina, and Texas, mitigation means the application of the latest building codes to the residential structures.[8]

Table 2.3 indicates the differences in losses and savings from adoption of mitigation measures for hurricanes with return periods of 100,

Table 2.3 Money Saved in Reduced Losses from Full Mitigation for Different Return Periods

	100-year event			250-year event			500-year event		
State	Unmitigated losses ($ billions)	Savings in reduced losses from mitigation ($ billions)	Savings in reduced losses from mitigation (%)	Unmitigated losses ($ billions)	Savings in reduced losses from mitigation ($ billions)	Savings in reduced losses from mitigation (%)	Unmitigated losses ($ billions)	Savings in reduced losses from mitigation ($ billions)	Savings in reduced losses from mitigation (%)
FL	84	51	61	126	69	55	160	83	52
NY	6	2	39	13	5	37	19	7	35
SC	4	2	44	7	3	41	9	4	39
TX	17	6	34	27	9	32	37	12	31

SOURCE: Kunreuther and Michel-Kerjan (2009).

250, and 500 years for each of the four states we are studying when these loss-reduction measures are in place. The analyses reveal that mitigation has the potential to reduce losses from future hurricanes by amounts ranging from 61 percent in Florida for a 100-year return period loss, to 31 percent in the state of Texas for a 500-year return period loss. In Florida alone, the use of mitigation leads to a $51 billion reduction in losses for a 100-year event and $83 billion for a 500-year event. These findings are important given the cost of capital needed to cover the tail of the distribution of extreme events. Adoption of mitigation measures on residential structures significantly reduces, if not eliminates, this tail in each of these four states.

The challenge, however, lies in making sure residents in hazard-prone areas invest in these mitigation measures. Indeed, recent extreme events have highlighted the challenges associated with reducing losses from hurricanes and other natural hazards due to what one of us has termed the natural disaster syndrome (Kunreuther 1996). Many home-owners, private businesses, and public sector organizations in hazard-prone areas do not voluntarily adopt cost-effective loss-reduction measures, making these areas highly vulnerable and unprepared should a severe hurricane or other natural disaster occur. The magnitude of the destruction following a catastrophe often leads governmental agencies to provide disaster relief to victims even if prior to the event the government claimed that it had no intention of doing so. This combination of underinvestment in protection prior to the catastrophic event and partial financing of the recovery by the general taxpayer can be critiqued on both efficiency and equity grounds.

A range of informal mechanisms explain this natural disaster syndrome. One relates to framing the problem imperfectly: experts focus on the likelihood and consequences as two key elements of the risk. Several studies show, however, that individuals rarely seek out probability estimates in making their decisions. When these data are given to them, decision makers often do not use the information. In one study, researchers found that only 22 percent of subjects sought out probability information when evaluating several risky managerial decisions. People have particular difficulty dealing with probabilistic information for small-likelihood events. They need a context in which to evaluate the likelihood of an event occurring. They have a hard time gauging how concerned to feel about a 1 in 100,000 probability of death without some comparison points. Most people just do not know whether 1 in 100,000 is a large risk or a small risk. In one study, individuals could not distinguish the relative safety of a chemical plant that had an annual chance of experiencing a catastrophic accident that varied from 1 in 10,000 to 1 in 1 million (Kunreuther, Novemsky, and Kahneman 2001).

There is also evidence that firms and residents tend to ignore risks whose subjective odds are seen as falling below some threshold. Prior to a disaster, many individuals perceive its likelihood as sufficiently low that they contend, "It won't happen to me." As a result, they do not feel the need to invest voluntarily in protective measures, such as strengthening their houses or buying insurance. It is only after the disaster occurs that these same individuals express remorse that they didn't undertake protective measures.

Individuals also do not invest in protective measures because they are highly myopic and tend to focus on the returns for only the next couple of years. In addition, there is extensive experimental evidence showing that human temporal discounting tends to be hyperbolic, so that events in the distant future are disproportionately discounted relative to immediate ones. As an example, people are willing to pay more to have the timing of the receipt of a cash prize accelerated from tomorrow to today than from the day after tomorrow to tomorrow (Loewenstein and Prelec 1991). The implication of hyperbolic discounting for mitigation decisions is that residents are expected to invest a tangible fixed sum now to achieve a future benefit that they instinctively undervalue—and that, paradoxically, they hope never to see at all. The effect of placing too much weight on immediate considerations is that the upfront costs of mitigation will loom disproportionately large relative to the delayed expected benefits from loss mitigation over time.

Extensive evidence indicates that residents in hazard-prone areas do not undertake loss-prevention measures voluntarily. A 1974 survey of more than 1,000 California homeowners in earthquake-prone areas revealed that only 12 percent of the respondents had adopted any protective measure (Kunreuther et al. 1978). Fifteen years later, there was little change despite the increased public awareness of the earthquake hazard. In a 1989 survey of 3,500 homeowners in four California counties at risk from earthquakes, only 5 to 9 percent of the respondents in these areas reported adopting any loss reduction measures (Palm et al. 1990). Burby et al. (1988) and Laska (1991) have found a similar reluctance by residents in flood-prone areas to invest in mitigation measures.

In the case of flood damage, Burby (2006) provides compelling evidence that actions taken by the federal government, such as constructing levees, make residents feel safe, when in fact they are still in harm's way should the levee be breached or overtopped. This problem is reinforced by local public officials who fail to enforce building codes or to impose land-use regulations to restrict development in high-hazard areas. If developers do not design homes to be resistant to disasters and individuals do not voluntarily adopt mitigation measures, one can expect large-scale losses following a catastrophic event, as evidenced by the property damage to New Orleans caused by Hurricane Katrina.

Even after the devastating 2004 and 2005 hurricane seasons, a large number of residents had still not invested in relatively inexpensive loss-reduction measures for their property, nor had they undertaken emergency preparedness measures. A survey of 1,100 adults living along the Atlantic and Gulf coasts conducted in May 2006 revealed that 83 percent of the responders had taken no steps to fortify their homes, 68 percent had no hurricane survival kit, and 60 percent had no family disaster plan (Goodnough 2006). As noted above, homeowners' failure to invest in cost-effective mitigation measures or to purchase adequate insurance coverage if not required to do so stems from behavioral and psychological biases. As a means to address these issues, we suggest the use of long-term contracts.

A NEW CONCEPT: THE DEVELOPMENT OF LONG-TERM INSURANCE CONTRACTS

We propose moving from the standard one-year insurance contracts for homeowners and flood insurance for residential properties to long-term insurance (LTI) to encourage property owners to invest in cost-effective mitigation measures.[9] In the case of homeowners coverage (which includes protection against the effects of wind damage, but not flood losses), some insurers have recently restricted the sale of new homeowners policies in hurricane-prone areas. Policyholders cannot help but worry that their existing coverage might be subject to unexpected cancellation or very significant premium increases, particularly if severe hurricane damage occurs in the near future.

Need for Long-Term Insurance

Short-term insurance policies foster significant social costs. Evidence from recent disasters reveals that consumers who fail to adequately protect their homes or even insure at all create a welfare cost to themselves and a possible cost to all taxpayers in the form of government disaster assistance. Under the current U.S. system, the governor of a stricken state can request that the president declare a "major disaster" and offer special assistance if the damage is severe enough. The number of presidential disaster declarations has dramatically increased over the past 50 years: there were 162 during the period 1955–1965, 282 during 1966–1975, 319 during 1986–1995, and 545 during 1996–2005 (Michel-Kerjan 2006).

The development of LTI should also encourage individuals to invest in cost-effective mitigation measures. As previously pointed out, many homeowners do not invest in such measures due to myopia and budget constraints. They are unwilling to incur the high upfront cost associated with these investments relative to the small premium discount they would receive the following year reflecting the expected reduction in annual insured losses (Kunreuther, Meyer, and Michel-Kerjan, forthcoming). If an LTI policy was coupled with a long-term home improvement loan tied to the mortgage, the reduction in insurance premiums would exceed the annual loan payment. LTI coupled with long-term mitigation loans over a number of years could yield significant social welfare benefits: less damage to property, reduction in costs of protection against catastrophic losses by insurers, more secure mortgages, and lower costs to the government for disaster assistance.

Why Does a Market for Long-Term Insurance Not Exist Today?

In his seminal work on uncertainty and welfare economics, Kenneth Arrow defined "the absence of marketability for an action which is identifiable, technologically possible, and capable of influencing some individuals' welfare . . . as a failure of the existing market to provide a means whereby the services can be both offered and demanded upon the payment of a price" (Arrow 1963). Here we shall discuss several factors that have contributed to the nonmarketability of LTI for protecting homeowners' property against losses from fire, theft, and large-scale natural disasters. We discuss elements that affect both the supply and demand sides.

Supply side

Today, due to political pressure, insurance rates are frequently restricted to be artificially low in hazard-prone areas, as illustrated by Florida's actions in recent years. As a result, the risks most subject to catastrophic losses also become the most unattractive for insurers. This premium regulation also results in a second stumbling block: insurers are uncertain how much they will be allowed to charge in the future. Uncertainty regarding costs of capital and changes in risk over time may also deter insurers from providing long-term insurance. In principle, of course, insurers could add a component in their premiums to account for the costs created by these factors. However, insurance regulators, presumed to be representing consumers' interests, may not allow these costs to be embedded in the approved premiums. Furthermore, it is unclear what the voluntary demand for coverage will be, given the resulting premiums. In a real sense, a new and less intrusive format for government regulation of insurance markets may be required if the private sector is to be successful in dealing with time-varying risks and capital costs.

Insurers might also be concerned about possible changes in the level of risk over time. For example, global warming could trigger more intense weather-related disasters, or local environmental degradation might change the risk landscape in the next several decades. One way to address this concern would be to make contracts renegotiable at a specified interval based on new information validated by the scientific community, much like renegotiable loans with adjustable rates (e.g., every five years).

Demand side

Some homeowners may worry about the financial solvency of their insurers over a long period, particularly if they are concerned about being locked into an LTI contract. Consumers might also fear being overcharged if insurers set premiums that reflect the uncertainty associated with long-term risks. Furthermore, those who have not suffered a loss for 10 years but have a 25-year LTI may feel that the premiums are unfairly priced. It is thus essential that the design of an LTI contract anticipate these concerns and be transparent to the policyholder.

Developing an LTI Policy

Jaffee, Kunreuther, and Michel-Kerjan (2008) have developed a simple two-period model in a competitive market setting, where premiums reflect risk, to compare the expected benefits of annual contracts versus LTI. The authors show that an LTI policy reduces the marketing costs for insurers compared with single-period policies, and also reduces the search costs to consumers if their insurer decides to cancel its policy at the end of period 1. If an LTI policyholder can cancel at the end of period 1 on learning that the cost of a 1-period policy is low enough to justify paying a cancellation cost (C), then it is always optimal for the insurer to offer an LTI policy and for the consumer to purchase one. The insurer will set C at a level that enables it to break even on those policies that are canceled before the maturity date. We should note that if one is going to develop any type of LTI policy that would be marketed by the private sector, then premiums need to reflect risk (Principle 1). If insurers can charge prices that enable them to break even, they will have incentives to develop new products. Under the current state regulatory arrangements, where many insurance commissioners have limited insurers' ability to charge risk-based premiums in hazard-prone areas, no insurance company would even entertain the possibility of marketing an LTI policy. Insurers would be concerned that the regulator would clamp down on them now or in the future regarding what price they could charge, so that a long-term contract would be infeasible from a financial point of view.

A NATURAL CANDIDATE FOR LONG-TERM INSURANCE: FLOOD INSURANCE THROUGH THE NFIP

Given the existing tension between state insurance regulators and the insurance industry, we feel that it is best politically to introduce LTI by focusing on flood insurance, since this coverage is provided by the federal government here in the United States. The National Flood Insurance Program (NFIP) was created in 1968 as a result of insurers' refusal to cover this risk because they viewed it as uninsurable. In 2007, the NFIP sold over 5.5 million policies (compared to 2.5 million in 1992) and covered over $1.1 trillion in assets (compared to only $237 billion in 1992). These figures were stable in 2008 (Michel-Kerjan and Kousky, forthcoming).

It would be useful to consider whether one could make flood insurance policies long-term by tying them to mortgages. This practice would connect insurance directly to the property, rather than to the homeowner. One might also consider requiring everyone in flood-prone areas to take out the insurance, just as those who own a car are required to take out automobile insurance today whether or not they are financing the purchase of their car. If a homeowner moved to another location, the flood insurance policy would remain with the property.

Why Have a Long-Term Flood Insurance Policy?

A long-term flood insurance program would offer homeowners currently residing in flood-prone areas a fixed rate for a fixed period of time (e.g., 5, 10, or 20 years). If the homeowner moved away from the area before the end of the policy period, then the insurance policy would automatically be transferred to the new property owner at the same rate. For those homeowners being charged subsidized rates because their homes were constructed before their community joined the NFIP, these rates would be maintained for the length of the policy period. For homeowners who constructed homes after their community joined the program, rates would be actuarially based.

For a number of reasons, such a long-term flood insurance policy would be a great improvement over the current annual policies from the perspective of the relevant stakeholders: homeowners, the Federal

Emergency Management Agency (FEMA), banks and financial institutions, and the general taxpayer. Assigning a fixed rate to flood insurance would provide financial stability to homeowners. They would also know that they are protected against water damage from floods and hurricanes. This would reduce the legal problems that have stemmed from recent hurricanes (such as the Florida hurricanes of 2004, Katrina, and Ike).

Long-term flood insurance would also ensure the spread of risk within the program, since most homeowners in flood-prone areas would be covered. Requiring flood insurance for all homeowners residing in hazard-prone areas would provide an even larger spread of risk. This larger policy base would provide much-needed financial revenue for the program over time.

Long-term policies would prevent individuals from canceling their policies after they have not experienced a flood for several years. Some individuals currently do this even if they are required to hold the policy as a condition for a federally insured mortgage. The banks and financial institutions have often not enforced this regulation because few of them have been fined or because the mortgages are transferred to banks in non-flood-prone regions of the country that have not focused on either the flood hazard risk or the requirement that homeowners may have to purchase this coverage. Consider the flood in August 1998 that damaged property in northern Vermont. Of the 1,549 victims of this disaster, FEMA found 84 percent of the homeowners in Special Flood Hazard Areas (SFHAs) did not have insurance, even though 45 percent of these individuals were required to purchase this coverage (Tobin and Calfee 2005).

If banks offered long-term loans for mitigation, individuals with long-term flood insurance policies would be encouraged to invest in cost-effective risk reduction measures. To highlight this point, consider the following simple example. Suppose a property owner's investment of $1,500 in floodproofing would reduce by $30,000 the water damage from a future flood or hurricane with an annual probability of 1 in 100. The NFIP should be willing to reduce the annual premium by $300 (i.e., $1/100 \times \$30,000$) to reflect the lower expected losses that would occur if a flood or hurricane hit the area. If the house was expected to last for 10 or more years, the net present value of the expected benefit of investing in this measure would exceed the upfront cost at an annual discount rate as high as 15 percent.

In the current system, many property owners would hesitate to make the $1,500 expenditure, because they would get only $300 back next year and might consider the benefits over only the next few years when making their decisions. If they underweight the future, the expected discounted benefits would likely be less than the $1,500 upfront cost. In addition, budget constraints could discourage them from investing in the mitigation measure. Other considerations that could play a role in the decision not to invest in these measures include uncertainty as to how long the family will reside in the house and whether their insurer would reward them again when their policy is renewed. There may also be a failure to appreciate the interdependencies associated with floods, earthquakes, and other disasters. That is, investing in mitigation measures can reduce not only the potential losses to one's own property but the damage to neighboring structures.

If a 20-year flood insurance policy was tied to the property, then the homeowner could take out a 20-year, $1,500 home improvement loan linked to the mortgage at an annual interest rate of 10 percent, resulting in payments of $145 per year. If the insurance premium was reduced by $300, the savings to the homeowner each year would be $155. Alternatively, this loan could be incorporated as part of the mortgage at an even lower interest rate than 10 percent.

Long-term insurance and mitigation loans would constitute new financial products. A bank would have a financial incentive to provide this type of loan, since it would be better protected against a catastrophic loss to the property, and the NFIP would know that its potential loss from a major disaster had been reduced. Moreover, this scenario would reduce the likelihood of large tax-dollar expenditures for disaster relief. Indeed, prior to the 2005 hurricane season, which inflicted nearly $18 billion in flood claims, the NFIP had a cumulative deficit of about $3 billion after 37 years of operation (Michel-Kerjan and Kousky, forthcoming). LTI thus offers a win-win situation for all.

CONCLUSION

Since the 1990s, a series of large-scale catastrophes have inflicted historic economic and insured losses. More than half of the 25 most costly insured catastrophes worldwide between 1970 and 2008 occurred after 2001, and all were natural disasters except for the 9/11 terrorist attacks. The United States has been particularly challenged, since 12 of these 25 disasters for insurance occurred in this country. The growing concentration of population and structures in high-risk areas, combined with the potential consequences of global warming, are likely to lead to even more devastating catastrophes in the coming years unless cost-effective risk reduction measures are put in place.

The challenge facing the United States and many other countries is ascertaining how to encourage residents and businesses to invest in loss-reduction measures and insurance in advance of a disaster so as to avoid the need for large-scale governmental disaster relief after a catastrophe occurs. Indeed, even when risk reduction measures are available and are cost-effective, many people are still not investing in them. Following a disaster, government agencies provide assistance to the area. We term this the natural disaster syndrome.

Several instances of the natural disaster syndrome have occurred in recent years. In the aftermath of Hurricane Katrina, many victims suffered severe losses from flooding because they had not used mitigation measures in their homes and did not have flood insurance to cover the resulting damage. The affected individuals and communities consequently received an unprecedented level of federal disaster assistance. There are many reasons why those in harm's way have not undertaken protective measures in advance of disaster. Many individuals believe that the event will not happen to them. In the case of New Orleans, some residents may have believed that they were fully protected by flood control measures such as the levees.[10] Such beliefs have led to increased development in hazard-prone areas without appropriate land-use regulations or properly enforced building codes. In addition, budget constraints and short time horizons may limit people's ability and desire to invest in hazard mitigation measures and to purchase insurance. Such a dynamic has been observed in many countries around the world.

We propose a new initiative that could address these issues: long-term insurance contracts coupled with long-term loans to encourage the adoption of cost-effective mitigation measures and provide stability to homeowners. Given the benefits and potential difficulties of implementing such a program, we conclude that flood insurance would be a natural candidate for such a long-term program. Given, too, that the NFIP is up for renewal in 2010, there may be the political will to develop more effective solutions.

There is an opportunity for the Obama administration and Congress to take steps now to reduce these losses and protect the nation against extreme events in a more systematic way than the government has to date. We need a more coherent national strategy for managing these risks in a new era of catastrophes.

Notes

This chapter was originally prepared for the American Enterprise Institute for Public Policy Research's conference "Private Markets and Public Insurance Programs," held at the Wohlstetter Conference Center, Washington, DC, January 15, 2009, and appears in *Public Insurance and Private Markets*, Jeffrey R. Brown, ed., AEI Press (2010). We would like to thank Jeffrey Brown, David Torregrosa, and other participants in the AEI conference for helpful comments on a previous version of this paper. We acknowledge support from the Wharton Risk Management and Decision Processes Center and a grant from the Federal Emergency Management Agency's Office of Preparedness Policy, Planning, and Analysis, a division of the National Preparedness Directorate, U.S. Department of Homeland Security (Grant #2008-GA-T8-K004). The views and opinions expressed are those of the authors and should not be interpreted as representing the U.S. government or FEMA.

1. It is quite remarkable that 2007 was the first year that the *Economic Report of the President* devoted a chapter to catastrophic risk insurance.
2. For a detailed analysis on terrorism insurance by the authors, see Kunreuther and Michel-Kerjan (2004), Wharton Risk Center (2005), Michel-Kerjan and Pedell (2006), and Michel-Kerjan, Raschky, and Kunreuther (2010). For a detailed analysis of the question of natural disaster insurance and mitigation in the United States, see Kunreuther and Michel-Kerjan (2009).
3. This figure excludes payment by the U.S. National Flood Insurance Program (NFIP) for damage due to 2005 flooding (over $20 billion in claims).
4. Munich Re and Swiss Re, the two leading reinsurers in the world, do not use the same definition of catastrophic losses. Natural disasters inflicting insured losses

above $38.7 million or total losses above $77.5 million are considered major catastrophes by Swiss Re. Munich Re uses a higher threshold, which explains the
difference between Figure 2.1 and Figure 2.2. For example, when Munich Re estimated insured loss from natural disasters at about $42 billion in 2004, Swiss Re's
estimate was over $52 billion.

5. These numbers vary depending on the definition of "coastal counties" one considers. The less restrictive definition, the one used for the figures in the text and
applying to 53 percent of the U.S. population, includes lakes. Taking a more restrictive definition (i.e., any county that has a coastline bordering the open ocean
or associated sheltered water bodies or a county that contains V zones—velocity
flood zones, or areas likely to have floodwaters of great velocity—as defined by
the National Flood Insurance Program), one still finds that the proportion of the
population living in such counties is 30 percent (Crowell et al. 2007).

6. For additional data on the economic impact of future catastrophic hurricanes, see
Rust and Killinger (2006), sec. 1:13–1:26.

7. For more details on the scientific evidence regarding climate change and its impact, see Stern (2007).

8. We are assuming that because these measures are incorporated in building codes
they are cost-effective. In other words, the discounted long-term expected benefit
from the mitigation measure over the projected life of the house is greater than its
upfront costs. By obtaining detailed cost estimates for specific mitigation measures incorporated in building codes or Florida's "Fortified . . . for safer living"
program, one could rank their relative cost-effectiveness.

9. This section draws heavily on Jaffee, Kunreuther, and Michel-Kerjan (2008).

10. FEMA clearly thought that the levees would provide this protection. Otherwise it
would have designated the Lower Ninth Ward as a hazard-prone area and residents
would have been eligible for flood insurance.

References

Arrow, K. 1963. "Uncertainty and the Welfare Economics of Medical Care."
American Economic Review 53(5): 941–973.

Association of British Insurers (ABI). 2005. *Financial Risks of Climate
Change*. London: Association of British Insurers.

Burby, R. 2006. "Hurricane Katrina and the Paradoxes of Government Disaster Policy: Bringing about Wise Governmental Decisions for Hazardous
Areas." *Annals of the American Academy of Political and Social Science*
604(1): 171–191.

Burby, R., S. Bollens, E. Kaiser, D. Mullan, and J. Sheaffer. 1988. *Cities under
Water: A Comparative Evaluation of Ten Cities' Efforts to Manage Floodplain Land Use*. Boulder, CO: University of Colorado, Institute of Behav-

ioral Science.

Council of Economic Advisers. 2007. *2007 Economic Report of the President.* Washington, DC: Council of Economic Advisers.

Crossett, K.M., T.J. Culliton, P.C. Wiley, and T.R. Goodspeed. 2004. *Population Trends along the Coastal United States: 1980–2008.* Silver Spring, MD: National Oceanic and Atmospheric Administration (NOAA), National Ocean Service, Special Projects.

Crowell, M., S. Edelman, K. Coulton, and S. McAfee. 2007. "How Many People Live in Coastal Areas?" *Journal of Coastal Research* 23(5): iii–vi.

European Commission. 2010. *Haiti Earthquake—EU Coordinates Aid.* Brussels: European Commission. http://ec.europa.eu/news/external_relations/ 100118_en.htm (accessed January 26, 2010).

Goodnough, A. 2006. "As Hurricane Season Looms, State Aims to Scare." *New York Times,* May 31, A:1. http://www.nytimes.com/2006/05/31/us/ 31prepare.html (accessed December 14, 2009).

Grossi, P., and H. Kunreuther, eds. 2005. *Catastrophe Modeling: A New Approach to Managing Risk.* New York: Springer.

Jaffee, D., H. Kunreuther, and E. Michel-Kerjan. 2008. "Long Term Insurance (LTI) for Addressing Catastrophe Risk." NBER Working Paper 14210. Cambridge, MA: National Bureau of Economic Research.

Kunreuther, H. 1996. "Mitigating Disaster Losses through Insurance." *Journal of Risk and Uncertainty* 12(2–3): 171–187.

Kunreuther, H., R. Ginsberg, L. Miller, P. Sagi, P. Slovic, B. Borkan, and N. Katz. 1978. *Disaster Insurance Protection: Public Policy Lessons.* New York: John Wiley and Sons.

Kunreuther, H., R.J. Meyer, and E. Michel-Kerjan. Forthcoming. "Strategies for Better Protection against Catastrophic Risks." In *Behavioral Foundations of Policy,* E. Shafir, ed. Princeton, NJ: Princeton University Press.

Kunreuther, H., and E. Michel-Kerjan. 2004. "Policy Watch: Terrorism Risk Insurance in the United States." *Journal of Economics Perspectives* 18(4): 201–214.

———. 2009. *At War with the Weather: Managing Large-Scale Risks in a New Era of Catastrophes.* New York: MIT Press.

Kunreuther, H., N. Novemsky, and D. Kahneman. 2001. "Making Low Probabilities Useful." *Journal of Risk and Uncertainty* 23(2): 103–120.

Laska, S. B. 1991. *Floodproof Retrofitting: Homeowner Self-Protective Behavior.* Boulder, CO: Institute of Behavioral Science, University of Colorado.

Loewenstein, G., and D. Prelec. 1991. "Negative Time Preference." *American Economic Review* 81(2): 347–352.

Michel-Kerjan, E. 2006. "Disasters and Public Policy: Can Market Lessons

Help Address Government Failures?" In *Proceedings from the Ninety-Ninth Annual Conference of the National Tax Association*. Washington, DC: National Tax Association, pp. 179–187.

Michel-Kerjan, E., and C. Kousky. Forthcoming. "Come Rain or Shine: Evidence on Flood Insurance Purchases in Florida." *Journal of Risk and Insurance*.

Michel-Kerjan, E., and B. Pedell. 2006. "How Does the Corporate World Cope with Mega-Terrorism? Puzzling Evidence from Terrorism Insurance Markets." *Journal of Applied Corporate Finance* 18(4): 61–75.

Michel-Kerjan, E., P. Raschky, and H. Kunreuther. 2010. "Corporate Demand for Insurance: An Empirical Analysis of the U.S. Market for Catastrophe and Non-Catastrophe Risks." Wharton Risk Center working paper. Philadelphia: Wharton School, University of Pennsylvania.

Mills, E., and E. Lecomte. 2006. *From Risk to Opportunity: How Insurers Can Proactively and Profitably Manage Climate Change*. Boston, MA: Ceres.

Munich Re. 2008. "Catastrophe Figures for 2008 Confirm That Climate Agreement Is Urgently Needed." News release, December 29. Munich: Munich Re. http://www.munichre.com/en/press/press_releases/2008/2008_12_29_press_release.aspx (accessed December 14, 2009).

———. 2009a. *Topics Geo—Catastrophes 2008*. Munich: Munich Re. http://www.munichre.com/publications/302-06022_en.pdf (accessed December 14, 2009).

———. 2009b. "Few Major Natural Catastrophe Losses in 2009: General Trend Confirmed by Large Number of Weather Extremes." News release, December 29. Munich: Munich Re. http://www.munichre.com/en/press/press_releases/2009/2009_12_29_press_release.aspx (accessed January 26, 2010).

Palm, R., M. Hodgson, R.D. Blanchard, and D. Lyons. 1990. *Earthquake Insurance in California: Environmental Policy and Individual Decision Making*. Boulder, CO: Westview Press.

Pielke, R. Jr., J. Gratz, C. Landsea, D. Collins, M. Saunders, and R. Musulin. 2008. "Normalized Hurricane Damage in the United States: 1900–2005." *Natural Hazards Review* 9(1): 29–42.

Rust, E.B., and K. Killinger. 2006. *The Financial Services Roundtable Blue Ribbon Commission on Mega-Catastrophes: A Call to Action*. Washington, DC: Financial Services Roundtable.

Stern, N. 2007. *The Economics of Climate Change: The Stern Review*. New York: Cambridge University Press.

Swiss Re. 2008. "Preliminary Swiss Re Sigma Estimates That Over 238,000 People Were Killed by Catastrophes in 2008, Insured Losses Soar to

USD 50 Billion." News release, December 18. Zurich: Swiss Re. http://www.swissre.com/pws/media centre/news/news releases 2008/pr_sigma _20081218.html (accessed December 14, 2009).
———. 2009. *Natural Catastrophes and Man-Made Disasters in 2008: North America and Asia Suffer Heavy Losses*. Zurich: Swiss Re. http://www .swissre.com/resources/dd6346004d4e9669ac76eecedd316cf3-sigma2 _2009_e.pdf (accessed December 14, 2009).
Tobin, R., and C. Calfee. 2005. *The National Flood Insurance Program's Mandatory Purchase Requirement: Policies, Processes, and Stakeholders*. Washington, DC: American Institutes for Research.
United Nations. 2004. *World Population to 2300*. New York: United Nations, Department of Economic and Social Affairs, Population Division. http:// www.un.org/esa/population/publications/longrange2/WorldPop2300final .pdf (accessed December 14, 2009).
Wharton Risk Center. 2005. *TRIA and Beyond: Terrorism Risk Financing in the U.S.* Philadelphia: Wharton School, University of Pennsylvania.

3
Expectations and Unexpected Consequences of Public Policy toward Natural and Man-Made Disasters

Anthony M. Yezer
George Washington University

For the purposes of this chapter, I define disasters very generally as large, sudden, infrequent occurrences that are difficult to forecast and that result in significant economic loss in the form of output, income, property, and life. Particular attention is given to disasters that are geographically concentrated as opposed to events like global depressions. This definition is broad enough to cover such disparate events as a regional recession, earthquake, hurricane, drought, oil spill, or terrorist attack.

A general approach to disasters has three advantages. First, the principle of parsimony holds that it is desirable to explain as many phenomena as possible with a single theory. Second, generality allows results developed for one type of disaster event to inform our thinking about the economic effects of other disaster types.[1] Third, models that claim to explain the effects of many different types of disasters are much easier to refute than those with few testable implications or with narrow predictive power. Theories that are easily refuted should inspire the strongest beliefs in other theories where there is an absence of successful refutation. Put another way, if someone advances a theory of the effects of Hurricane Katrina and claims that it is uniquely appropriate for the U.S. Gulf Coast, the theory is not likely to be generally useful and, because it is based on a single data point, its ability to account for the effects does not indicate that the findings on which it is based are statistically significant.

Literature on the economic effects of disasters concentrates on measures of direct and indirect effects. Direct effects are losses associated with observable damage to property, production, and persons. Indirect effects are costs of recovery and mitigation efforts. Indirect costs are more difficult to observe but can be and have been well measured. This chapter concerns itself with effects that arise through changes in expectations. Direct observation of expectations is generally either not possible, too expensive, or not precise. Accordingly, expectations models must generate a number of implications that can provide indirect validation of the underlying theory.

Three disaster expectations models are examined in this paper. First, and most direct, is the effect of disaster expectations on local property values and economic development. Particular attention is given to the possibility that recent disaster experience changes local disaster expectations. This model implies that economic effects of disaster events are based on the unanticipated component of disaster events, or on the difference between actual and expected disaster losses. Second, the effect of disaster expectations on incentives to develop land is considered. Using models taken from urban economics, it is possible to demonstrate circumstances under which private returns from development of land in hazard-prone areas are less than social returns. Third, disaster expectations of property owners should include not only direct damage to their own assets but also the possibility of asset revaluation due to the external effects of disasters on surrounding property. The findings demonstrate that expectations regarding these external effects make disaster insurance different from other forms of hazard insurance and explain some puzzles about behavior of property owners in disaster-prone areas.

The next four sections of the chapter discuss these three models of disaster expectations (the direct effect of disaster expectations is analyzed in two sections). The final section summarizes the major findings and develops implications of these models for understanding the likely effects of changes in public policy toward natural and man-made disasters.

INDIVIDUAL AND MARKET RESPONSES TO DISASTER EXPECTATIONS

There is ample evidence that disaster expectations are priced into markets. The most obvious example is insurance against disaster events, where pricing is based on sophisticated models of the likelihood that events will occur and the estimate of damage, conditional on the event happening. Those insurance companies that do not price insurance and accumulate reserves using statistical models of disaster expectations do not remain solvent for long and can generally be dismissed as curiosities that have no long-term importance.[2]

There is a strong argument that competitive pressures force most firms to form and act upon efficient disaster expectations, because they must purchase hazard insurance in order to secure capital investment. However, the case for household responses to disaster expectations is not so obvious. Indeed, there is evidence that households are reluctant to purchase insurance against disaster events even when the insurance is subsidized. Before discussing models that trace the effect of disasters on the economy through their effect on disaster expectations, it is worth reviewing the evidence on household responses to disaster expectations.

Because disasters are infrequent and difficult to forecast, households will have difficulty forming expectations regarding their likelihood and severity. However, the literature on individual responses to other large, low-frequency hazards appears to conclude that the implied value of life based on household mitigation behavior is consistent and not unreasonable.[3] This suggests that households may have reasonable disaster expectations. Shilling, Benjamin, and Sirmans (1985) find that households, confronted with different hazard insurance rates associated with location within or near a floodplain, require a compensating differential in housing prices to live in areas where the expected cost of flood damage is larger. MacDonald, Murdoch, and White (1987) carry the analysis further by modeling the relation between house price discounts and the discounted present value of future insurance payments and conclude that, at reasonable discount rates, housing price differentials reflect differences in expected future insurance premiums.

Thus far the evidence discussed deals with cases in which static differences in disaster expectations influence household behavior. Research has also been done on the effects of changes in disaster expectations due to the provision of expert information. Brookshire et al. (1985) examined the effects on housing prices of the requirement that home sellers in California reveal proximity of the housing unit to earthquake fault lines. The regulation was passed based on the belief that this information was not available to buyers. The natural experiment, with observations before and after the information and for houses in and out of the fault areas, indicated that the proximity to the fault line affected price after the announcement was made.[4]

Perhaps the most dramatic demonstration of the economic effects of disaster information was the response to federal government notices of earthquake hazards in the resort community of Mammoth Lakes, California, from 1980 until 1984. The unique feature of this incident was that the United States Geological Survey (USGS) recognized that making public announcements of changes in the probability of seismic events could have serious consequences and implemented an experimental design around the pronouncements. The USGS adopted a three-level index of potential hazard and, from 1980 to 1984, announced seismic risks for Mammoth Lakes that began with the lowest and ended at the highest risk level. The results of this experiment, as reported in a detailed study by Bernknopf, Brookshire, and Thayer (1990), were dramatic. Surveys of the resident population showed that there was a substantial increase in perceptions that a seismic event was likely after each announcement of increasing risk. Recreational use of the area did not fall. However, new construction and house values fell significantly. The market response was so dramatic that the USGS decided to abandon its three-level seismic hazard announcement policy.[5]

Overall, there is substantial empirical evidence that firms and households have significant market responses to information on the likelihood of hazard events, whether that information is presented in the form of insurance rates or government announcements. This should not come as a surprise, and the economic effects of these reactions are easily understood and consistent with economic efficiency. When increased hazard expectations are capitalized into the asset price of real property, construction in hazard-prone areas is discouraged and property owners have an incentive to adopt designs that mitigate the likely damage should a disaster occur. All this is unsurprising and well established in the literature. Indeed, there is nothing in the foregoing discussion that distinguishes market reactions to disasters from the economics of hazards generally.

THE ECONOMIC EFFECTS OF CHANGES IN DISASTER EXPECTATIONS

Because disasters are infrequent, large, spatially concentrated, and difficult to forecast, there is a possibility that disaster events change disaster expectations, and, of course, that failure to experience disasters changes expectations in the opposite direction. This is a distinguishing characteristic of disasters.

Hazards that are not infrequent, large, spatially concentrated, or difficult to forecast have expectations that are not significantly influenced by individual hazard events. The fact that a house in a neighborhood burns down has zero effect on insurance models or public expectations of fire damage hazards. This is true because home fires are frequent, impose modest losses, are not spatially concentrated, and can be forecast with great precision. Individual occurrences of an event that is fairly likely to happen have little effect on the expected probability of that event.

Because disasters are infrequent and difficult to forecast, firms and individuals should use recent history to update their expectations of the stochastic process generating the disasters. This was very evident in the reaction to hurricane losses in Florida during the 1990s when property insurance companies raised rates or withdrew from the market, necessitating the formation of a government-sponsored Florida Hurricane Catastrophe Fund. This is one of many examples in which it appears evident that an increase in the frequency or extent of disaster events causes insurance companies to modify stochastic models of disaster loss and substantially raise insurance premiums. The natural presumption is that firms and households behave similarly and that in addition to the direct and indirect effects of disasters, disaster events have an expectations effect due to the consequences of the modified estimates of disaster losses. Such effects might well have negative implications for recovery and growth of income, output, population, and so on.

There is contradictory evidence regarding the effect of disasters on expectations based on the relation between disaster experience and economic development. In a very influential statistical analysis of disaster events, Wright et al. (1979) concludes that the rates of growth are higher after disasters than before and that long-run growth is higher in areas that experience disaster events. An extensive literature has compared economic outcomes in areas with and without disaster events. Most recently, Belasen and Polacheck (2008) apply a generalized difference in difference estimator to counties in Florida over the 1988 to 2005 period, when the state experienced 19 major storms. They find that employment fell by about 4.8 percent and total earnings rose 4.4 percent in counties experiencing direct hits, while total earnings fell 4.5 percent in neighboring counties. These differences dissipate over time. Studying international disasters, Cuaresma, Hlouskova, and Obersteiner (2008) find evidence that countries with higher disaster rates experience higher rates of subsequent economic growth.[6] Further evidence presented by Worthington (2008) indicates that natural disaster events have no significant effects on overall stock market returns. These and a large number of other statistical studies of cross-section and panel data on areas with and without disaster events tend to produce evidence that disasters are not associated with significant negative effects on output, earnings, and employment. One or more of these variables may decline, but the type of general negative implication for economic growth that would be expected from an upward revision in disaster expectations has not been observed.

There is a parallel literature consisting of case studies conducted in the aftermath of disasters. Dacy and Kunreuther (1969) contend that the rush of aid in response to the great Alaskan earthquake of 1964 gave an area in long-term decline a chance to reverse its falling employment. Other case studies have reached similar conclusions. Recently Smith et al. (2006) found that the recovery pattern from Hurricane Andrew varied by income group, with the numbers of high- and low-income households growing in the aftermath of the storm while the number of middle-income households fell. While case studies of the aftermath of

Katrina are not available yet, it appears certain that income, output, and employment will not recover. Still, the general sense of the literature reviewed above is that the answer to the question, "Are disasters bad for economic growth?" could be "no" or at least "not necessarily." This leads to the subsequent question, "Is postdisaster relief too generous?"

There is a problem with both of these questions as well as the proposed answer. Understanding the problem and formulating an answer will require development of a formal model of the likely effects of changed disaster expectations on economic growth. The model begins with an understanding of real estate values in an urban land market. Because real estate is immobile, differences in future expectations for regional economic activity tend to be capitalized in land and housing values. There is a well-developed literature on quality of life stemming from the work of Rosen (1974) and Roback (1982, 1988) that suggests a relation among amenity, house prices, and wages in a labor market area. Decreases in amenity are associated with increases in wages and decreased house prices in order to keep households from leaving an area. A rise in disaster expectations makes an area less attractive to both firms and households. Under these circumstances the change in wages is ambiguous because there is a spatial no-arbitrage condition for firms based on profits and for households based on indirect utility.[7] However, the theory unambiguously predicts that land and real estate prices will fall in response to an increase in disaster expectations.

Rubin and Yezer (1987) provide a general empirical test of the relation between disaster events and local economic activity by examining the change in house prices in areas experiencing different numbers of disasters. For a panel of U.S. cities in 1983, they analyzed the partial effect on the asset prices of housing, as reported in the American Housing Survey for a cross-section of cities, in relation to differences in the number of disaster events during the previous 20 years.[8] The estimated coefficient of disasters was positive, and its magnitude implied that going from an annual disaster rate of zero to one increased the value of owner-occupied housing in the city by 26 percent.[9] The authors point out that such an interpretation of the estimated coefficient of disasters is absurd, and they argue from these results that something is very wrong with models that relate the incidence of disaster events to local economic development.

The literature has documented the effects of information from insurance pricing, scientific evidence, and government pronouncements on disaster expectations. It is much more difficult to determine the effect of disasters themselves on disaster expectations. This is perhaps the most underresearched aspect of the economics of disasters. A disaster event might lower, raise, or leave unchanged disaster expectations of a rational agent, depending on the nature of the disaster. Some seismic events occur periodically and, given the slow pace of geologic time, an eruption today may mean that the next eruption is hundreds of years in the future. Alternatively, recent storm damage may lead individuals to expect that the underlying frequency of storms has increased due to global climate change.

This paper is particularly concerned with the case in which, given the complexity or lack of information on the process generating the disaster, agents update their expectations of the frequency distribution of disasters based on a comparison of recent disaster experience with the historical record. Such updating may occur for two reasons. First, individuals may believe that the disaster-generating process varies over time and may be trying to estimate the parameters of a stochastic process with drift.[10] Alternatively, they may believe that disasters are generated by a stationary stochastic process and simply use recent experience to improve their estimates of the parameters of that distribution. Because this second case is easier to describe and has been analyzed in the literature, it will be considered in some detail here.

In considering the case of a stable stochastic process, the Poisson process is quite attractive because it requires individuals to estimate a single parameter, and the probability of a disaster event is independent of the time since the last disaster. Cox and Lewis (1966) first suggested fitting the Poisson process to disaster events, and Brown (1972) adapted it to the case of flooding. Analysis of Bayesian updating of expectations regarding the Poisson process is mercifully simple. The process is based on a single parameter: the expected disaster frequency, f. The expected time between disasters, T, is the reciprocal of f; that is, $T = 1/f$. Assume that the historical record available at time t indicates that α disasters were observed over the previous τ years. Then the estimate of f at time t is simply the ratio $f_t = \alpha / \tau$. Now assume that, in the next X years, β additional disasters occur. Then the Bayesian estimate of f at time $t + X$ is $f_{t+X} = (\alpha + \beta) / (\tau + X)$. The change in estimated disaster frequency between t and $t + X$ is given by

$$\Delta f = f_{\tau+x} - f_{\tau} = [(\alpha + \beta)/(\tau + X)] - [\alpha / \tau]$$

$$= [\beta/(\tau + X)] - [\alpha /(\tau + X)](X/\tau)$$

$$= [\beta - \alpha(X/\tau)]/(\tau + X).$$

This final expression has a very intuitive interpretation. The change in expected disaster frequency is equal to the difference between actual disaster experience during the recent period of X years, β, and expected number of disasters based on the previous τ years, $\alpha(X/\tau)$, divided by the total number of years under consideration, $X + \tau$. Thus this change represents the difference between actual and expected disasters per year of disaster history available to the individual making the estimate.

Rubin and Yezer (1987) discuss whether the difference between actual and expected disasters could help explain the more rapid increase in house prices in cities that had more disasters. Dividing the 20-year period over which presidential disaster declarations were observed in their cross-section of cities into a 16-year "history" that served as the basis for estimates of disaster expectations and a subsequent 4 years of recent experience, they computed the difference between the number of actual and expected disasters in the recent period and reestimated the model of house price change discussed above. The disaster rate for the entire period still had a positive sign, but the difference between actual and expected disasters (i.e., the number of unexpected disasters) had a substantial negative effect on house values.

How should these results be interpreted? It appears that during this period, cities where disaster expectations were higher were growing faster than those where disaster expectations were lower. Given that cities with higher disaster expectations have more disasters, this produced a positive association between house price growth and the disaster rate. This association is of no particular significance unless there is further evidence that the growth of cities in areas with higher disaster rates is being subsidized. Put another way, the literature on the relation between area economic growth and disaster frequency does not reveal the effects of disasters on growth because most disasters are anticipated. Development takes place in high-disaster areas only in anticipation of future damage, and that expected damage is part of the cost of doing business in those areas. "What is the effect of disasters on economic growth?" is a vexed question. The appropriate question is, "What is the effect of unanticipated disasters on economic growth?"

The effect of unanticipated disasters on house values found by Rubin and Yezer (1987) is substantial. Consider an area that had no previous disaster experience and then had one disaster during the four-year event window; that is, it had one unanticipated disaster. This would lower house values by 2 percent. This change may not seem large; however, in a city with 500,000 housing units with an average value of $200,000, the change in expectations due to the single unanticipated disaster event lowers total house values by $2 billion! This is only one example of how the effects of unanticipated disasters can be large compared to the direct damage and indirect recovery costs.

The implications for public policy of these substantial effects on local economies of changes in disaster expectations based on disaster events will be discussed in some detail in a subsequent section. It should be clear that disasters that have the same direct and indirect effects in terms of damages to property, income, output, and individuals have very different long-term local effects depending on the extent to which they were anticipated. Furthermore, while it is possible, at least in theory if not in practice, to insure against direct and even some indirect losses due to disaster events, insuring against losses due to changed expectations is impossible. Indeed, it is likely that firms and households in areas with high disaster expectations are well insured against direct and indirect losses, whereas those in areas where expectations are low are unlikely to insure against these insurable losses. Thus the overall uninsured losses from unanticipated disasters are likely to be very large. It should also be obvious that the economic effects of man-made disasters, particularly acts of terrorism, are best understood in terms of changes in expectations.[11] Other things being equal, those terrorist acts that produce damages of a type or in a location where expectations were low have the largest economic effects. These considerations will prove very important in the discussion of policy implications.

Disaster Expectations and Efficient Land Use and Mitigation

Most of the literature on disaster expectations and efficient economic development deals with excess development and insufficient mitigation efforts in areas where disaster frequencies are high. This problem has been the object of congressional testimony and reports as well as academic inquiry.[12] Once disaster relief became a regular and mandated part of federal policy, there was an incentive for states, localities, and individuals to self-insure development in hazardous areas. The normal disincentives to such development—namely, the prospect of loss and the cost of insurance—were mitigated by the prospect of postdisaster relief.[13] Concern over this problem has led to a number of initiatives, including the National Flood Insurance Program, which dealt with excess development and inadequate mitigation by combining disaster relief provisions with mandatory insurance and design requirements. The Coastal Zone Management Act of 1972 promoted state and local planning efforts to control and direct development, and the Coastal Barrier Resources Act of 1982 attempted to deter development by cutting off federal funding to designated areas that had high disaster probability and environmental sensitivity.

The general sense of the literature appears to be that government policy for disaster relief is subject to the Samaritan's dilemma: these efforts create major problems of moral hazard, adverse selection, and time inconsistency that encourage development and discourage mitigation in disaster-prone areas.[14] Mandatory insurance, design controls, mandatory mitigation, and even designation of areas in which government assistance will not be provided are generally seen as the proper response to the distortions produced by disaster relief programs.

This section focuses on an issue that has attracted negligible interest in the literature: spatial land market models suggesting that there is too little development in areas where disaster expectations are high. The overdevelopment literature discussed above tends to ignore issues of space and location that are governed by the functioning of the land market. Because land subject to high disaster risk is spatially concentrated, the development of significant areas is contingent on the treatment of disaster losses. Frame (1998, 2001) has considered this issue explicitly, as follows. Take the land market in a standard urban model in which land at a particular location has special value based on unique locational advantages, such as the central business district of a city or a shoreline location. For simplicity's sake call this the high-productivity area. Land rents will peak at such points and decline with distance. What happens if some of the land at or near the peak of this land rent surface is not developed because it is subject to flooding or some other hazard that would inflict substantial damage on real property? Frame demonstrates that this undeveloped land yields a general loss of community welfare because the area as a whole is less efficient at providing developed sites with access to the high-productivity area. This result holds even if the high-hazard area does not impede through access; for example, if the area lacks housing but highways can be built through it to transport workers or consumers from distant points to the high-productivity area.

More recently Liu (2008) has examined the relation between the private and social returns from developing land in and around high-productivity areas. The private gain from developing land in hazardous areas is the difference in value between undeveloped and developed land. Part of the development process is the opportunity for mitigation, and the assumption is that insurance markets are available or that developers are risk-neutral. His results are quite intuitive. If there are no externalities associated with the functioning of a perfectly competitive land market, private benefit from development of land subject to hazards is equal to the social benefit, and private land market allocations are socially efficient. However, if there are externalities in the operation of the land market, particularly problems of traffic congestion, social benefit can be significantly larger than private benefit. Using a numerical urban simulation model with congestion calibrated to Kansas City, Liu finds that the social value of development near central city areas is approximately twice the private benefit realized by the land owner.[15] This means that land subject to hazards could have too little development. McDonald (2009), in a similar model calibrated to Chicago, confirms the general result that, in the presence of congestion, private benefits to development of land near the central business district are significantly below social benefits. While he does not relate these results to effects of hazards, the arguments made here would hold in his model also.[16]

Nothing in this discussion of the land market models and the possibility of underdevelopment of high disaster risk areas should be seen as a contradiction of the literature on incentives for excess development due to moral hazard arising from federal disaster relief programs.[17] However, land market efficiency considerations do suggest that, in some circumstances, there are countervailing forces that tend to restrict development below optimal levels in areas that are prone to disasters. Accordingly, such areas should be given careful attention to determine which of the conflicting forces is larger.

Disaster Expectations, External Effects, and Disaster Insurance

One puzzle in the disaster literature involves the reluctance of households in high-risk areas to purchase insurance even if the price appears to be below expected losses. The failure to use subsidized insurance has troubled many observers. Kunreuther (1978) noted that, in the first four years of the National Flood Insurance Program (1968–1972), only 3,000 of 21,000 eligible communities with substantial flooding history participated in the program, and fewer than 300,000 homeowners voluntarily purchased a policy. Even though the NFIP was subsidized, participation was initially achieved only by threatening to withhold federally assisted or guaranteed construction from nonparticipating communities, and by denying mortgage loans to property owners in nonparticipating communities that were identified as special flood hazard areas.[18] Palm et al. (1990) documented a similar failure of homeowners and mortgage lenders to seek earthquake insurance in high-risk areas. Kunreuther and Kleffner (1992) and Kunreuther (1996) have even argued that homeowners do not behave as if they are maximizing expected utility in their decisions to purchase insurance or engage in private mitigation efforts.

The discussion of disaster insurance is generally conducted using models standard in the insurance literature. A household owns an asset whose current value is A which is subject to expected damages of D_A so that its expected value in the next period is $A - D_A$ with variance V_D. The variance in $A - D_A$ is due to the possibility that the hazard event might occur during the current time period. Given that the expected value of damage due to the hazard is generally known to be D_A, the household can purchase hazard insurance at a price of $D_A + F$, where F is the normal fee associated with providing this insurance product under perfect competition. Households have a choice of purchasing full insurance or no insurance. What are the consequences for wealth in the next period? Expected wealth under full insurance is $A - (D_A + F)$, with certainty compared to expected wealth of $A - D_A$ with variance V_D without insurance. Insurance reduces the variance in return to zero because the insurance payment is perfectly correlated with the damage to asset value. Households that are moderately risk averse will choose insurance, and there is no reason to assume that households owning property in disaster-prone areas are not moderately risk averse.[19] This line of argument has treated disaster risk the same as other risks to property, such as fire, liability, collision, or theft.

One distinguishing characteristic of disasters, as defined in this essay, is the extent and spatial concentration of damage. In terms of the simple example above, any damage to asset value A is likely associated with damage experienced by the full alphabet of asset values owned by other households in the area. In this case, the fall in wealth experienced by the household is equal to $A - (D_A + E_A)$, where E_A is the external effect of disaster damage to other properties in the area on the value of the asset. Assume that V_E and r_{ED} are the variance of E and the correlation between E and D respectively. A household that purchases insurance has expected wealth of $A - (D_A + F + E_A)$ with variance V_E, and the household that self-insures has expected wealth of $A - (D_A + E_A)$ and variance of $(V_D + V_E)/2 + r_{ED} (V_E V_D)^{0.5}$. The variance in second-period wealth of those who purchase insurance depends crucially on r_{ED}. Consider the stylized but not unreasonable case in which V_D is equal to V_E and r_{ED} equals one, so that the external damage is perfectly correlated with the damage to the structure. Then the variance becomes $2V_D$ and the risk of self-insuring has doubled. In this case, the household has the choice between two risky alternatives but, again abstracting for other opportunities for risk diversification, the moderately risk-averse household is likely to have a risk premium greater than F and will choose to purchase insurance. Now consider the other extreme, in which V_D is equal to V_E and r_{ED} equals -1. The household that self-insures has expected second-period wealth of $A - (D_A + E_A)$ and variance of zero. This household thus will rationally self-insure unless insurance is heavily subsidized. Indeed, there is a separating equilibrium for r_{ED} sufficiently small that even very risk-averse households switch from buying to not buying insurance.

The incentive to purchase insurance and the effects of mandatory insurance depend on the relative sizes of D_A and E_A and particularly on the sign and size of r_{ED}. Given that the indirect effects of disasters take the form of a local public good, it may appear that this correlation is positive and close to one. However, one line of argument suggests r_{ED} is negative. If a structure is damaged but the damage is less than that of surrounding structures, then the rental price of its services may well rise because the disaster reduces the supply of real property for a significant period after the event. Furthermore, the reduction in real property may be permanent.

Perhaps the most obvious case for a negative r_{ED} is that of beach property located in the third or fourth row of homes from the shoreline. In most beach communities, there is a sharp decline in value as distance from the shoreline increases: that is, value varies inversely with row. In storm events, most damage is experienced by the first and second rows. In some cases, the first row cannot be rebuilt due to shoreline erosion, and each subsequent row then moves up the value gradient. Put another way, the third row is one large hurricane away from being beachfront property.

This simple model illustrates that, if there are significant external effects that are negatively correlated with private damages, the effect of insurance on economic development becomes rather complex. As noted above, many property owners will fail to insure even if insurance pricing is based on shared expectations of future damages. The provision of such insurance benefits those owners whose expected external effects are either small or positively correlated with private damages. It does not benefit owners with large external effects that are negatively correlated with damages. Therefore, mandating disaster insurance for all property owners imposes net costs on owners of properties with significant external effects that are negatively correlated with damages. This leads to the surprising result that mandatory purchase requirements for insurance that is priced based on expected damages distorts asset prices and property development by lowering asset prices for properties with large external effects that are negatively correlated with damages.

The example noted of beach property in different rows may offer a test of the theoretical arguments made above. The nature of external effects should vary significantly with distance from the shoreline. Given that the hazard is storm damage by wind and waves, it is likely that private damage in the first row will be much larger than any external effects and that external effects will be positively correlated with damages.[20] Moving back to the second and third rows of property, these relative effects are likely to be reversed. Shoreline erosion may imperil the first row, but it simply makes inland areas more proximate to the beach. Damages to interior areas are very likely to be smaller than in the first row. Overall it appears that shoreline areas provide an excellent natural experiment to assess the varying importance of private damages versus external effects for economic activity.

The difficulty with testing the effects of private damage and external effects on investment in beach property is that the test requires differentiating among rows of beach development: that is, the geographic scale is very small. Testing for insurance effects is further complicated because the current NFIP has been in place in most beach communities since the mid-1980s, so insurance coverage has not varied significantly in recent years. The most direct way to measure effects of insurance coverage is to look for capitalization in asset prices by monitoring the variation in house values by row and over time. Some research on the effects of government policy on beachfront residential development has been done using hedonic house value equations (Keeler, Kriesel, and Landry 2003), repeat sale house price indexes (Cordes, Gatzlaff, and Yezer 2001), and building permits issued (Cordes and Yezer 1998). Unfortunately, none of these techniques is suitable for tracking development effects on shoreline property based on distance in feet from the water's edge in beach communities over the period extending from before the NFIP through its current form. Such an analysis would require price or permit data going back to 1968 differentiated by row from the shoreline. No such data are available.

Cordes, Yezer, and Asadurian (2008) found another way to test for the differential effects of flood insurance by row from the beachfront. Property records include the number of square feet of interior space of dwellings and the date that the housing was built. Using aerial photographic maps, they were able to divide beach developments into rectangles corresponding to development rows whose land area is fixed and measurable. Using building records that gave the number of square feet of interior space in each dwelling in a rectangle, it was possible to construct a time series going back to 1968 of the square feet of interior space per square foot of land area, commonly known as the "floor/area ratio." The result of this effort was a 40-year time series of the capital/ land ratio in each rectangle for the period from 1968 to 1997. The maps also facilitated calculation of distance of each row from the water's edge and, together with information on erosion rates, this allowed computation of estimated time until erosion undermined the structures in a given rectangle.[21]

Each beachfront community entered into the NFIP in two stages. First it entered the emergency program, where flood insurance was heavily subsidized, and then, after completion of a flood insurance map (FIRM), it entered the regular program, in which insurance subsidies for new construction were much smaller or nonexistent.[22] Given that the various communities entered these two phases in different years, the data include observations of communities with and without each of the programs in any given year as well as before and after information for each community. The estimation results demonstrated that entering both the emergency and regular NFIP had the effect of tilting real property development toward the shoreline. The rate of growth in density, measured as floor/area ratio, increased the most in the first row, but this positive effect fell off rapidly, reaching zero at a distance of 350 feet from the water's edge. The effect was large, statistically significant, and congruent with the theoretical prediction that programs mandating insurance encourage development in areas where the external effects of hazards are negligible or positively correlated with the private damage—the first rows of shoreline development. At the same time, mandatory insurance programs discourage development in areas where the external effects of hazards are large or negatively correlated with private damage—rows located inland.

Thus it appears that the existence of expectations that disasters are associated with both private damage and external effects creates the paradoxical possibility that mandating universal purchase of insurance based on expected private damage estimates distorts the location of economic activity toward areas where expected hazard losses are higher. While this may appear counterintuitive, it does explain the difficulty in getting some households in high-risk areas to participate in the NFIP.

IMPLICATIONS OF DISASTER EXPECTATIONS FOR PUBLIC POLICY

Formal models of the economic effects of natural and man-made disasters should include careful modeling of expectations, because the prior level of disaster expectations, and any resulting changes in the expectations, are very important determinants of those economic effects. This essay has developed some of the pathways relating expectations and economic effects, but other important linkages in need of research may exist. Nevertheless, the analysis presented here is sufficient to demonstrate some important principles whose implications for public policy toward disasters will be discussed, including the effects of changed disaster expectations, efficient land use considerations, and potential distortions due to mandated insurance and mitigation.

Changes in Disaster Expectations

The economic effects of disasters depend on the relation between prior expectations and actual disaster experience. This is illustrated in the literature on the effects of earthquakes on property values and disaster expectations. Beron et al. (1997) find that property values near fault lines actually rose after the Loma Prieta earthquake and argue that prior expectations were too high. In contrast, Naoi, Seko, and Sumita (2009) report that for earthquakes in Japan, surveys show that quake expectations double after an event and property values fall significantly. If actual disasters reflect disaster expectations, then those expectations will be unchanged and negative expectations' effects on economic development should be minor. The economic effects of a disaster depend not only on how much damage it does but also the extent to which the disaster event and the associated damage were anticipated. Furthermore, it is not possible for firms and households to insure against the economic losses associated with changed expectations after unanticipated disasters. What does this imply for public policy? First, it suggests that insurance markets are inherently incomplete and that there is a role for postdisaster aid. However, the aid should be focused on areas experiencing unanticipated disaster events.

While such selective targeting of disaster relief to unanticipated disasters is likely politically impossible, some elements of disaster relief policy seem consistent with a focus on events that raise expectations. First, there is a scale effect in disaster declarations, so larger disasters get proportionally greater postdisaster compensation.[23] To the extent that unusually large disaster events are unanticipated, making federal participation a nonlinear function of the size of the aggregate losses is appropriate. Furthermore, NFIP aid diminishes for repeated flooding events. The subsidized insurance for grandfathered structures can be withdrawn after repeated losses. Finally, the amount of publicity and attention given to disaster events may decrease to the extent that the event is regular and anticipated. This may lower the amount of public and private aid following such events. Certainly, more could be done with formal policies toward postdisaster aid to concentrate public funds on unanticipated disaster events, but in this case political expediency likely will triumph over economic logic.

Another implication of the losses associated with unanticipated disasters is that terrorists who wish to inflict maximum total damage for a given amount of physical damage will concentrate their actions where damage is not anticipated. There are many other considerations in selecting targets, but areas where disaster expectations are low have two advantages. First, victims will likely not be taking precautions. This makes success in inflicting damage more likely, and perhaps also lowers the probability of apprehension and sanction if that is a consideration. Second, the unexpected component of the disaster event is largest in areas where prior expectations are lowest. In this case the implications for public policy are clear and, fortunately, the politically expedient course does not tend toward moral hazard. Provision of generous relief from damages lowers the expectation of loss from man-made disasters. This lowers the economic effects because the economic reaction will depend both on the change in expectations of the probability of loss and on the expectation of the size of loss conditional on the act taking place.

Relief can do nothing about the change in probability, but it can lower the conditional expectation of loss and hence the economic effects produced by the change in expectations.[24]

Incentives for Efficient Land Use and Mitigation

The moral hazard and time inconsistency problems associated with federal provision of disaster relief are well understood.[25] Indeed, the cornerstone of disaster policy since the passage of NFIP has been to resolve the Samaritan's dilemma by forcing those developing property in hazardous areas to face an insurance price that reflects expected future losses and required mitigation to control those losses. Insurance and mitigation costs, in turn, discourage development.

Because hazards are spatially concentrated, public policy toward disasters has an important effect on when and how densely significant tracts of land are developed. When this issue is considered in terms of a continuous land market model, it is important that the private incentives to develop land in hazardous areas be consistent with the social benefits from such development. If land is homogenous, private benefit equals social benefit and private landlords should develop land only when the private returns to development are sufficient to compensate for the cost of development, including any expected disaster losses. However, all land is not homogenous, and there may well be externalities associated with land development, particularly in an urban setting where accessibility is important and transportation systems are congested. Under such circumstances the social benefit from developing sites may exceed the private benefit, and landlords may fail to develop land or may do so at a density that is below the social optimum. In these circumstances, public action to subsidize mitigation or insurance can be justified.

There are many examples of public policy efforts to subsidize development of hazard-prone land in an urban context. Many communities have used general public funding for flood control and land reclamation efforts.[26] The arguments made in this essay suggest that there is an economic rationale for these actions and that public subsidy calls for a demonstration of social benefits in excess of private benefits. In cases where subsidized mitigation is not feasible or not economical, provision of subsidized insurance can also align private and social benefits from development. Such policies must be implemented with some care, because political abuse by subsidizing development where there is no externality is also possible.

External Effects and Disaster Insurance

Because disaster effects are spatially concentrated, the usual insurance model should be applied cautiously in developing the economic effects of disaster insurance. When disaster strikes, owners of property suffer private damage and insurance compensates for those losses. Insurance is also available for some of the disruption following the disaster—that is, for the indirect effects of the disaster. It is easy to construct an argument for mandatory participation in an actuarially sound disaster insurance program, particularly when the government is committed to providing relief services.

This argument ignores external effects of disasters on asset prices in an area. One can easily identify situations in which these external effects are positive and offset the private losses. This explains why some property owners in hazardous areas rationally fail to purchase hazard insurance, even when the insurance is subsidized. Public policies that mandate purchase of actuarially fair insurance in such cases will distort the pattern of economic development toward areas where expected private losses are high compared to any external effects. These may well be the areas where disaster damage expectations are highest. The end result could be to encourage the movement of economic development into harm's way.

This does not mean that it is necessary to abandon public policies of mandating the purchase of disaster insurance. It does suggest that the case for mandating purchase should be very strong. In such cases, it should be possible to provide insurance at rates that are higher than actuarially fair in areas where external effects are positively correlated with private losses and at a discount to fair rates where external effects are negatively correlated with private losses. Identification of these areas need not involve substantial economic analysis: they should be apparent based on patterns of participation in voluntary insurance programs or even in our current "mandated" programs by observing areas where actual participation rates are either very high or very low.

Overall, models that integrate expectations of natural and man-made disasters into the body of economic theory suggest that public policy toward these events needs to be carefully considered. The great difficulty facing the federal government is the general presumption that programs and policies need to be nationally uniform. Considerations of economic efficiency appear to run counter to this presumption.

Notes

1. There is currently a national need to understand the effects of terrorist events. In the absence of the ability to extend results from other types of disasters to terrorism, this understanding would have to wait for a significant number of terrorist incidents to accumulate to provide a database suitable for testing. This is not a happy prospect.
2. This is not to say that the consequences of failure to price risk correctly are uninteresting or unimportant. Surely the credit default insurance industry of the past decade has had large negative economic effects, and so the "solution" to risk can itself result in a disaster event if that solution is unsound. These issues are beyond the scope of this paper, which assumes that insurance pricing is based on the latest and best estimates of risk.
3. See, for example, the recent discussion by Hakes and Viscusi (2007).
4. In this case proximity to a fault line was not indicated by insurance rates in ways that would make it apparent to home buyers. Indeed, the provision of earthquake insurance in California has been problematic for some time now for reasons that would easily justify an essay of considerable length.
5. The subsequent absence of a seismic event of any size proved embarrassing to the USGS, and there were threats of litigation by property owners.
6. The conclusion is somewhat more nuanced, as the authors find that the higher growth rate postdisaster depends on the initial economic circumstances of the country.
7. A rise in disaster expectations lowers expected profits or raises insurance costs for firms, which then require compensation in the form of lower wages and/or lower rents. The same rise lowers indirect utility of households, and they require compensation in the form of higher wages and/or lower rents. The change in wages is ambiguous but rents, and hence property values, must fall.
8. Specifically, they estimated a standard hedonic model for the logarithm of house value explained by a variety of housing characteristics standard in the literature but with area disasters added.
9. A disaster event is defined as one that resulted in a presidential disaster declaration. The disaster variable is the number of disaster declarations in the previous 15 years divided by 15 to produce an annual rate.
10. Recent attention to climate change may lead individuals to believe that the frequency of disasters is changing. Whether this belief is scientifically valid or not,

those who hold it will be updating based on an underlying stochastic model that allows for drift. Further research on this possibility is warranted.

11. These statements are based on an implicit model in which the supply of terrorist acts is elastic. Models with a fixed supply of terrorist events, such as those described in Barker (2003), may result in different implications than those discussed in this paper.

12. For an extensive discussion see Congressional Research Service (1992).

13. See, for example, the analysis in Shilling, Benjamin, and Sirmans (1985).

14. Moral hazard arises in the form of the Samaritan's dilemma. Individuals fail to insure or mitigate because they expect government postdisaster relief. Adverse selection problems occur if individuals with unrealistic expectations for disaster probabilities selectively migrate to hazardous areas. The time inconsistency problem arises when individuals believe that, by moving to a hazardous area, they can prompt public expenditures to mitigate the hazard by governments anxious to conserve on disaster relief cost. In other words, move onto the floodplain and the government will be forced to build a dam or levee at public expense.

15. Congestion in commuting is endogenous in this model. Given highway capacity, the model generates congestion based on the number of individuals choosing to commute through a particular segment of the city.

16. Chicago presents an interesting historical case because the portion of the city north of Lake Street is built on fill land that was created to realize the high social return of filling in the shore of Lake Michigan.

17. In addition to the standard arguments about excess development in high-risk areas already discussed, there is a more general literature on excess investment in real property, particularly second homes, based on the tax preference for owner-occupied housing; see Poterba and Sinai (2008).

18. While the subsidy component of NFIP insurance for new construction is not large, the subsidy for existing units built before the insurance was implemented is very large. Furthermore, lenders are required to check for flood insurance in connection with mortgage servicing. Kriesel and Landry (2004) report survey evidence indicating that the participation rate is only 49 percent in spite of the mandate that mortgage servicers require evidence of insurance in force.

19. Evidence for the degree of risk aversion could be gleaned from portfolio behavior of households based on property ownership. It has been argued that perception of risk from hazards is selectively faulty or that households owning property in areas with high disaster probability are selected to be those who systematically underestimate the hazard.

20. Damages in interior areas may impede recovery and repair in shoreline areas as well as raise the cost of these activities.

21. Obviously, beach erosion can sometimes be zero or even negative, i.e., the beach is accreting. In such cases estimated erosion time is infinite. The areas considered in this study are all beaches and subject to erosion. They are not protected by natural or man-made barriers. The potential for storm damage is substantial in these areas.

22. New construction was also subject to special construction requirements designed to raise vulnerable structures above flood surge levels.

23. Note that there is an element of size needed even to qualify for a presidential disaster declaration.
24. To the extent that the object of terrorism is to produce the greatest economic dislocation possible through the expectations effect, lowering the expectations effect reduces the returns to terrorism.
25. For an early discussion of these issues along with an estimate of the wealth redistribution effects of the NFIP, see Shilling, Sirmans, and Benjamin (1989).
26. The reclaimed land is then sold back to the private sector at a loss. Policy toward urban brownfields follows a similar pattern.

References

Barker, David. 2003. "Terrorism Insurance Subsidies and Social Welfare." *Journal of Urban Economics* 54(2): 328–338.

Belasen, Ariel R., and Solomon W. Polacheck. 2008. "How Hurricanes Affect Wages and Employment in Local Labor Markets." *American Economic Review* 98(2): 49–53.

Bernknopf, Richard L., David S. Brookshire, and Mark A. Thayer. 1990. "Earthquake and Volcano Hazard Notices: An Economic Evaluation of Changes in Risk Perceptions." *Journal of Environmental Economics and Management* 18(1): 35–49.

Beron, Kurt J., James C. Murdoch, Mark A. Thayer, and Wim P. M. Vijverberg. 1997. "An Analysis of the Housing Market before and after the 1989 Loma Prieta Earthquake." *Land Economics* 72(1): 101–113.

Brookshire, David S., Mark A. Thayer, John Tschirhart, and William D. Schulze. 1985. "A Test of the Expected Utility Model: Evidence from Earthquake Risks." *Journal of Political Economy* 93(2): 369–389.

Brown, John P. 1972. *The Economic Effects of Floods: Investigations of a Stochastic Model of Rational Investment Behavior in the Face of Floods.* New York: Springer-Verlag.

Congressional Research Service. 1992. "A Descriptive Analysis of Federal Relief, Insurance, and Loss Reduction Programs for Natural Hazards." Washington, DC: Congressional Research Service.

Cordes, Joseph J., Dean H. Gatzlaff, and Anthony M. Yezer. 2001. "To the Water's Edge and Beyond: Effects of Shore Protection Projects on Beach Development." *Journal of Real Estate Finance and Economics* 22(2–3): 287–302.

Cordes, Joseph J., and Anthony M. Yezer. 1998. "In Harm's Way: Does Federal Spending on Beach Enhancement and Protection Induce Excessive Development in Coastal Areas?" *Land Economics* 74(1): 128–145.

Cordes, Joseph J., Anthony M. Yezer, and Alis Asadurian. 2008. "Flood Insurance, Coastal Erosion, and Beachfront Development." Working paper. Washington, DC: George Washington University, Center for Economic Research.

Cox, D. R., and P.A.W. Lewis. 1966. *Statistical Analysis of a Series of Events.* London: Methuen.

Cuaresma, Crespo J., Jaroslava Hlouskova, and Michael Obersteiner. 2008. "Natural Disasters as Creative Destruction? Evidence from Developing Countries." *Economic Inquiry* 46(2): 214–226.

Dacy, Douglas C., and Howard Kunreuther. 1969. *The Economics of Natural Disasters: Implications for Federal Policy.* New York: Free Press.

Frame, David. 1998. "Housing, Natural Hazards, and Insurance." *Journal of Urban Economics* 44(1): 93–109.

———. 2001. "Insurance and Community Welfare." *Journal of Urban Economics* 49(2): 267–284.

Hakes, Jahn K., and W. Kip Viscusi. 2007. "Automobile Seatbelt Usage and the Value of a Statistical Life." *Southern Economic Journal* 73(3): 659–676.

Keeler, Andrew, Warren Kriesel, and Craig Landry. 2003. "Expanding the National Flood Insurance Program to Cover Coastal Erosion Damage." *Journal of Agricultural and Applied Economics* 35(3): 639–647.

Kriesel, Warren, and Craig Landry. 2004. "Participation in the National Flood Insurance Program: An Empirical Analysis for Coastal Properties." *Journal of Risk and Insurance* 71(3): 405–420.

Kunreuther, Howard. 1978. *Disaster Insurance Protection: Public Policy Lessons.* New York: John Wiley and Sons.

———. 1996. "Mitigating Disaster Losses through Insurance." *Journal of Risk and Uncertainty* 12(2–3): 171–187.

Kunreuther, Howard, and Anne E. Kleffner. 1992. "Should Earthquake Mitigation Measures Be Voluntary or Required?" *Journal of Regulatory Economics* 4(4): 321–333.

Liu, Feng. 2008. "Interrupted Development." Working paper. Washington, DC: George Washington University.

MacDonald, Don, James C. Murdoch, and Harry L. White. 1987. "Uncertain Hazards, Insurance, and Consumer Choice: Evidence from Housing Markets." *Land Economics* 63(4): 361–371.

McDonald, John. 2009. "Calibration of a Monocentric City Model with Mixed Land Use and Congestion." *Regional Science and Urban Economics* 39(1): 90–96.

Naoi, Michio, Miki Seko, and Kazuto Sumita. 2009. "Earthquake Risk and Housing Prices in Japan: Evidence before and after Massive Earthquakes." *Regional Science and Urban Economics* 39(6): 658–669.

Palm, Risa I., Michael E. Hodgson, R. Denise Blanchard, and Donald I. Lyons. 1990. *Earthquake Insurance in California: Environmental Policy and Individual Decision-Making.* Boulder, CO: Westview Press.

Poterba, James, and Todd Sinai. 2008. "Tax Expenditures for Owner-Occupied Housing: Deductions for Property Taxes and Mortgage Interest and the Exclusion of Imputed Rental Income." *American Economic Review* 98(2): 84–90.

Roback, Jennifer. 1982. "Wages, Rents, and the Quality of Life." *Journal of Political Economy* 90(6): 1257–1278.

————. 1988. "Wages, Rents, and Amenities: Differences among Workers and Regions." *Economic Inquiry* 26(1): 26–41.

Rosen, Sherwin. 1974. "Hedonic Prices and Implicit Markets." *Journal of Political Economy* 82(1): 34–55.

Rubin, Claire B., and Anthony M. Yezer. 1987. *The Local Economic Effects of Natural Disasters.* Working Paper 61. Boulder, CO: University of Colorado, Institute of Behavioral Science.

Shilling, James D., John D. Benjamin, and C. F. Sirmans. 1985. "Adjusting Comparable Sales for Floodplain Location." *Appraisal Journal* 53(3): 429–436.

Shilling, James D., C. F. Sirmans, and John D. Benjamin. 1989. "Flood Insurance, Wealth Redistribution, and Urban Property Values." *Journal of Urban Economics* 26(1): 43–53.

Smith, V. Kerry, Jared C. Carbone, Jaren C. Pope, Daniel G. Hallstrom, and Michael E. Darden. 2006. "Adjusting to Natural Disasters." *Journal of Risk and Uncertainty* 33(1–2): 37–54.

Worthington, Andrew C. 2008. "The Impact of Natural Events and Disasters on the Australian Stock Market: A GARCH-M Analysis of Storms, Floods, Cyclones, Earthquakes, and Bushfires." *Global Business and Economics Review* 10(1): 1–10.

Wright, James D., Peter H. Rossi, Sonia R. Wright, and Eleanor Weber-Burdin. 1979. *After the Cleanup: Long-Range Effects of Natural Disasters.* London: Sage.

4

The Economics of Disaster

Retrospect and Prospect

Hal Cochrane
Colorado State University

In preparing this chapter, I initially wrote that the economics of hazards and disaster is a subfield of environmental economics. Upon reflection, I crossed that out, replacing it with "the economics of hazards is a subfield of no less than five major fields, including behavioral economics, finance, regional economics, public finance, and environmental economics." This of course made the retrospective a bit daunting, especially for a chapter of this length. So, in looking back over the last 40 years, I culled a few key ideas that were influential in shaping disaster research over this formative period.

When it came to providing a prospective view, I took the easy path. I limited my coverage to the field that has absorbed my efforts over the past 30 years: that is, the regional and national economic consequences of disaster.

SOME HISTORY

The beginnings of this field can be traced back as far as John Stuart Mill, who, I am embarrassed to admit, preempted much of what I will present in the second half of the paper. Nearly 150 years ago Mill remarked about the economics of disaster, commenting on "what has so often excited wonder, the great rapidity with which countries recover from a state of devastation; the disappearance, in a short time, of all traces of the mischiefs done by earthquakes, floods, hurricanes, and the ravages of war" (quoted in Hirshleifer 1987, p. 79).

Almost a century later, John Kenneth Galbraith corroborated Mill's observations. As director of the Strategic Bombing Survey, Galbraith investigated the impact of Allied bombing raids on the German war machine. The survey concluded that the raids had had little impact. Hamburg recovered nearly 80 percent of its productive capacity within several months after a series of devastating attacks. The bombing raids virtually decimated the city's infrastructure, killed nearly 40,000 people and destroyed 50 percent of the city's buildings (Hirshleifer 1987). Despite these losses, production was only modestly affected.

These early roots provide a glimpse of the field's beginnings. However, it wasn't until the 1960s that four publications helped launch the field: *The Economics of Natural Disasters: Implications for Federal Policy* (Dacy and Kunreuther 1969), *Design of Water-Resource Systems* (Maass et al. 1962), *A Unified National Program for Managing Flood Losses* (U.S. Congress 1966), and "Losses from Natural Hazards" (Russell 1970). Dacy and Kunreuther provided key insights into the economic consequences of disasters (in this case the 1964 Alaskan earthquake). *Design of Water-Resource Systems* set down the procedures for conducting benefit-cost studies of water projects. *A Unified National Program for Managing Flood Losses* encouraged the adoption of a wider range of flood mitigation measures (at least wider than the system of levees and reservoirs the Corps of Engineers had promoted prior to that time) and introduced the idea that flood insurance *might* serve as a mechanism to promote an efficient means of coping with flood hazards. The word *might* is emphasized since the document was wary about insurance, for it was pointed out that an improperly structured insurance program could make things worse. These three publications provided enough starter material to employ a (very) small army of economists for the next 40 years.

From what I gather, Cliff Russell's classic "Losses from Natural Hazards" grew out of his association with the Harvard Water Resources Program and his collaboration with Bob Kates. This association was key since Bob Kates, Gilbert White, and Ian Burton are widely recognized as the field's pioneers. Russell's piece served to convert the basics of water resource economics into the economics of hazard management. In short, he showed that protection from natural events should be adopted so long as the expected marginal benefit (the loss avoided due to protection) exceeded the expected marginal cost of that protection. In hindsight this is not a startling finding, and a direct line can be drawn back to Harvard, particularly the work of Arthur Maass, Maynard M. Hufschmidt, Robert Dorfman, Harold A. Thomas Jr., Stephan A. Marglin, and Gordon Maskew Fair. Despite its simplicity, the idea proved to be a powerful reminder that hazards management involves a balance between costs and losses.

It could be said that Russell's work was foreshadowed by two earlier papers, one by Lester Lave (1963) and the other by Richard Nelson and Sidney Winter (1964). Although their work did not address hazards in the way that Russell did, the framework developed served as a foundation for later work in managing a wide range of hazards. There is of course much more to the story. But a recurring theme in all these works is the interplay of costs and losses, either objective or perceived. The retrospective segment of the paper will thus focus on a few key ideas that grew out of this early body of work. The second part, the prospective view, will concentrate on new avenues of research involving disaster loss. This, in my view, is perhaps the most important yet least understood aspect of the problem.

RETROSPECT

As indicated earlier, there is a vast body of literature to plow through in order to come up with a set of key ideas. Much of what I am about to present is based on the works of Lave (1963), Nelson and Winter (1964), and Howe and Cochrane (1976). All three investigate whether to mitigate losses from a potentially damaging event. They conclude (as did Russell) that the interplay of event probabilities and subsequent consequences shapes that choice. The framework about to be presented draws upon a highly stylized example, one where floods are of a dichotomous nature, and costs, losses, and event probabilities are well known. The presentation assesses the merits of taking action (or not) in view of a short-term flood forecast. It then entertains the possibility that it might be economically advantageous to adopt a more permanent flood mitigation strategy, one that is tied to the probability of flooding alone, ignoring forecasts altogether. Finally, the framework is tweaked to address very long-run changes in climate.

The purpose of this exercise is to demonstrate the power of these simple models. Although not very complex, nor pathbreaking, they offer policymakers valuable insights into how to value meteorological forecasts and even climate change research.

The Value of Forecasts

Should one heed a flood forecast? The answer to this question hinges on the cost of doing something, the loss incurred if a flood occurs (and insufficient protection is afforded), the climatological record, and the accuracy of the forecast. To illustrate, let's begin by characterizing flooding as a dichotomous event: it either occurs or it doesn't (Figure 4.1). Four combinations of flood forecasts and events are shown in Figure 4.1. When forecasts are perfect, P3 and P4 equal zero. But forecasts may be in error; predicted floods fail to materialize, and unpredicted

Figure 4.1 Decision to Adopt Forecast-Sensitive Protection

Probabilities

		Flood forecast	
Flood	No	P1	P2
	Yes	P3	P4

Consequences

		Flood forecast	
Flood	No	0	$C_{short\text{-}run}$
	Yes	Loss	Loss, $C_{short\text{-}run}$

NOTE: Adopt short-run protection if $C_{short\text{-}run} \times (P2 + P4) + Loss \times P3 < Loss \times (P3 + P4)$.
SOURCE: Author's calculations.

floods occur. The situation can be visualized as one where sandbags can be added to the levee provided that sufficient lead time is afforded. Whether such a forecast should be used hinges on the expected sum of costs and losses. It makes economic sense to adopt protection and use the forecast if the expected cost of sandbagging, C(P2 + P4), is less than the expected loss, L(P3 + P4).

The Value of Long-Term Protection

One might wonder whether there is a better way to deal with the hazard; a more permanent form of protection might be more efficient. In this case flood forecasts are disregarded in favor of probabilities dictated by the climate. Here the cost of protection is certain and the expected loss is the probability of flooding times loss. Note that these losses and costs are likely to be different from those shown in Figure 4.1, but the interplay of cost and loss is key to adopting protection nonetheless: that is, adopt long-run protection if $C_{long-run}$ < L(P3 + P4).

A Simple but Powerful Way of Conceptualizing the Hazard Problem

This highly simplistic framework provides some very useful insights into the value of information. One is that it is not always wise to act on a forecast. Errors might be too costly, and doing nothing may be the most economical path. This point is easily demonstrated by asking what a hail forecast is worth to a wheat farmer. Since there are no technically feasible ways of protecting the crop from damage, it follows that the forecast would be worthless (perhaps less than worthless since the farmer would worry about the fate of the crop). The framework also raises the issue of perceptions versus objective measures. If the decision maker is ill equipped to assess the probabilities (as Howard Kunreuther has often pointed out) or does not take into account the full magnitude of losses and costs, then the choice observed will not be the optimal choice. Finally, the value of improving disaster forecasts is a dynamic metric: it hinges on how losses and cost change over time. This may seem a bit abstract, but consider that the current climate change debate revolves around escalating losses observed along the nation's coastline. At first blush, rising losses could be interpreted to mean that the probabilities have shifted. However, it is just as likely that both the coastal population and the wealth at risk have risen over the past 50 years. The framework just presented allows for either or both. Roger Pielke Jr. (2005) performed a careful analysis of hurricane losses and concluded that rising losses are tied to population and wealth and not to increased frequency and severity. Although there is still a healthy debate about the issue (Emanuel 2005), the cost-loss framework has proven useful in pointing research in the right direction.

A Deeper Look at the Economics of Climate Change

The cost-loss model also lends itself to a deeper analysis of climate change. Although the problem still involves cost, loss, and the probability of disaster, the interpretations are different. The cost of mitigating the effects of climate change is the reduction in economic growth resulting from curtailing CO_2 emissions. The economics of cap-and-trade are pretty clear: investments in cleaner-burning fuels and higher-cost renewables will ratchet growth downward. The cost to GDP is open to debate, but few will argue that the difference in growth paths is the cost of capping emissions. The loss incurred in the event of climatic warming is just as contentious. But much of the debate revolves around the magnitude of loss. There is considerable disagreement regarding the degree to which the climate will change, and predictions of the economic impacts are therefore equally murky. Despite this, no one is arguing that climate change will be benign. If we assume for argument's sake that climate change losses will be disastrous and that anthropogenic CO_2 is in fact the chief culprit, a case can be made for controlling emissions now. Assume that $P_{anthropogenic}$ is the current assessment regarding the likelihood that anthropogenic CO_2 is the chief cause. Assume too that if emissions are curtailed now, future losses would be mitigated. On the other hand, if no action is taken to control atmospheric carbon, and CO_2 is indeed the causal agent triggering a more varied climate, the decision to do nothing will be irreversible. In contrast, the decision to limit fossil fuel use now can be revisited once the results of climate research become more definitive. This option is reversible if at some later date it is revealed that atmospheric carbon is the product of warming and not the other way around. In the economics literature the benefit of taking action now that may be revised later when updated information is available is referred to as quasioption value. The factors underlying this decision are the same as those that shaped the use of climate and weather information in the previous cost-loss example. Carbon control is worthwhile if the losses are sufficiently high, the control costs low, and the *a priori* probabilistic assessment of the connection between CO_2 and climate change is high. That is, the decision to curtail anthropogenic CO_2 is optimal if $C_{control}/L_{disaster}$ < $P_{anthropogenic}$. Despite its simplicity, the framework provides a valuable guide for debating climate policy. First, a good case can be made for taking action now despite the uncertainties regarding the causal mechanism. Waiting until these uncertainties are resolved could be the least appealing option. The decision to act now hinges on the cost, the losses, and the current state of knowledge regarding the direction of the causal arrow—that is, the probability that the arrow representing causation points from anthropogenic CO_2 to climate (i.e., anthropogenic CO_2 is causing climate change) rather than from climate to CO_2. Second, the framework properly draws attention to the role of anthropogenic CO_2 rather than to warming itself.

PROSPECTIVE VIEW OF LOSSES

It is clear from the preceding retrospective that losses (either objectively measured or perceived by the decision maker) are crucial to managing natural hazards. However, what constitutes a loss and how losses should be measured remain murky. Before we look at losses in more detail, it is worth taking a moment to reflect on the possibility that the market may have already discounted for locational risk. In other words, the price of housing might already accommodate the location of the property in an area subject to some hazard. If it does, then there is no reason to proceed any further. There has been some debate about this, but in my opinion it is highly unlikely that prospective buyers are well informed about risks of any sort. Howard Kunreuther has spent the better part of his career arguing that decision makers make poor choices because they use simple heuristics. In some cases they totally ignore low-probability events, and in others they overstate the likelihood of high-consequence events. The market for housing (and willingness to pay) reflects this. However, if market prices reflect considerable ignorance and misinformation, it is unwise to utilize them to formulate policy. The recent housing market collapse serves to illustrate this point quite nicely. Despite what orthodox economists claim for the market, I believe, at least for natural hazards, that housing prices provide little useful information regarding willingness to pay for safety. Loss studies are so important precisely because markets provide such unreliable information.

So, what losses are we talking about and how should they be measured? As will be discussed shortly, loss consists of the obvious (damage to buildings, contents, infrastructure, as well as loss of life) and the not-so-obvious (loss of cultural icons, historic monuments, a sense of place, and the indirect economic dislocations stemming from damage). Table 4.1 provides a simple list. I will address each briefly and then move on to regional and national economic impacts, which I will address in more detail.

Property Losses and Deaths

There is a substantial body of work tying wind velocity, ground shaking, and flood depth to property damage and subsequent loss of life. Although empirically estimated damage functions contain a substantial error band, they seem to work fairly well, particularly when damages are aggregated over a wide area. The Federal Emergency Management Agency's HAZUS program (Hazards United States), a sophisticated geographic information system, incorporates such functions for a variety of building types and hazards. In my view, property loss is the least problematic of all the losses. Similarly, there appears to be an empirically verifiable linkage between fatalities and the number of structures destroyed, at least for sudden-onset events such as tornadoes and earthquakes. Thus damage and fatality seem reasonably predictable through available means. The same cannot be said about the other categories of loss I am addressing, including value of life.

The value of a life

Although deaths are predictable, the value attached to each death remains an elusive concept. I realize that this is a highly contentious topic fraught with technical and ethical complexities. Having said that, I want to raise a few issues. Most important, disaster mortality and morbidity models account for statistical lives lost, not identified lives. No one worries about insurance companies that project loss of life and attempt to quantify those losses. An identified life is something quite different, however. No one would or should attempt to assess the value of an identified life. Second, if we are unwilling to attach a value to these so-called statistical deaths, then we might finesse the question by determining how much it costs to preserve a life through protective measures such as land use regulation and improved building codes. It is then up to the public to determine whether the costs are worth it. The benefits of hazard mitigation would have to be weighed against other life-saving options (e.g., dialysis, wellness programs). Although the problems inherent in estimating and valuing loss of life are formidable, they are relatively manageable.

Loss of cultural icons and historic monuments

While a solid foundation exists for the debate over mortality and direct damage to property, the state of knowledge regarding the other losses shown in Table 4.1 pales in comparison. Value is inherent in cultural icons, historic monuments, and a sense of place. Hurricane Katrina did more than destroy the city of New Orleans. The nation lost a cultural heritage that was rich in diversity and steeped in history. Much that has been written about post-Katrina New Orleans bemoans the changes wrought by the storm. The losses suffered go beyond the number of

Table 4.1 An Analysis of Losses

Mortality, morbidity, along with property damage are the best known.

Loss of environmental services, cultural icons, historic monuments, and a sense of place are less well known and understood.

Systemic risk and loss of regional economic activity are also not well understood.

deaths and the damage to buildings inundated because of breached levees, and even beyond New Orleans itself to affect the nation as a whole. Despite the growing body of literature attempting to establish values for nonmarket losses, measurement of iconic value remains a problem. Icons and monuments have market values that are readily measurable through surveys and travel-cost methods. However, such techniques don't reveal their existence value. Research on this rich and intriguing subject is still in its infancy.

Systemic and indirect losses

Systemic and indirect losses are also not well understood. The current financial panic has served to rivet attention on just how large contagion effects and their associated indirect impacts can be. Furthermore, the current economic meltdown underscores an important point. That is, the loss anticipated by any one participant can turn out to be vastly different when interindustry linkages and uncertainty are considered. Or, as Gary Becker said in addressing the 2008 financial meltdown, "While financial specialists understand how individual assets function, even they have limited understanding of the aggregate risks created by the system" (Becker 2008).

This observation bears directly on the cost-loss framework developed earlier, and on willingness to pay for protection. The events of late 2008 and early 2009 have underscored the point that an individual's perceptions are often at odds with systemwide risks. Given this discrepancy, it seems again unwise to rely on market forces to suggest a meaningful measure of willingness to pay for safety. I will spend the remainder of the paper on this topic, emphasizing the likely economic consequences of disaster, how to measure them (including why commonly utilized techniques fail), and why the results of some disasters differ significantly from those of others.

Alternative Ways of Modeling the Regional Economic Response to Shocks

There is currently no clear consensus as to how supply shocks can be successfully modeled. Input-output models have been tried, as have a wide range of alternatives, including computable general equilibrium models, econometric models, and even postevent surveys. They all leave something to be desired. A lot of what I will be discussing relies on a basic understanding of input-output models. A brief discussion of input-output basics is provided in Appendix 4A for those unfamiliar with the technique and its terminology.

Input-output models were designed to explain how final demand changes ripple throughout a region's (or nation's) interconnected sectors. The linkages are rather straightforward. An increase or decrease in demand for one sector's production indirectly boosts or reduces demand for ingredients supplied by other sectors. As a result, a one-dollar change in demand leads to more than one dollar's change in production when all intermediate transactions are accounted for. Input-output models have one fatal limitation: they are incapable of addressing the types of bottlenecks commonly observed after disaster. These models have no way of accounting for the possibility that supplying sectors may lack the capacity to provide needed inputs (leading to forward-linked losses) or, conversely, that producing sectors may lack the capacity to absorb all that their suppliers wish to ship (causing backward-linked losses).

Since the input-output technique implicitly assumes that there are no limits to production, it is incapable of treating the uneven set of supply constraints typically observed after disaster. It would be purely coincidental if the pattern of economic disruption emerging after a natural disaster matched the pre-event production pattern. Therefore, altering final demands to fit postdisaster production patterns would be problematic.

The other techniques just mentioned also have limitations. Computable general equilibrium models (CGEs) are an elaborate form of input-output, with an interindustry table at the core. CGEs permit final demand substitutions as shortages materialize. Unfortunately, the estimates of substitution elasticities embedded in the CGEs are problematic at best, particularly for unique events such as natural disasters. Furthermore, in some cases where a public utility is impacted (such as a water treatment or supply system), there is no meaningful measure of substitutability. CGEs are less useful for that type of loss estimation.

Finally, a shortcoming of both econometric models (particularly time series) and postdisaster surveys is that they are calibrated using a set of unique events. Time series techniques, like *event analysis*, look at the difference between trends with and without a disaster. Although appealing on the surface, event analysis is applied to *an* event. Since it is *an* event, it reflects only the characteristics of that event: the disaster relief policies in place, the pattern of destruction, the nature of the economy, and so on. Therefore, it is difficult to generalize from such an analysis to other potential events. Because of this limitation, event analysis may be useful for forensic studies, but not for policy analysis. A similar criticism applies to postevent surveys. What can one say beyond what the survey indicates about the loss sustained by a particular place, given that it was struck by a particular event at a time when a particular set of disaster relief policies applied? Very little.

An Algorithm for Analyzing Supply Shocks

An algorithm was developed at Colorado State University to address the shortcomings of the approaches just discussed. As in the case of CGE, the algorithm takes a region's interindustry linkages as its core. It then allows for excess capacity in each sector as a function of the region's rate of unemployment. Furthermore, the algorithm augments internal production with the aid of imports from other regions. Finally, it allows for the stimulative effects of reconstruction spending and the fiscal drag caused by indebtedness. The algorithm then seeks out the best outcome (in terms of regional income) that rebalances the economy. The economy is rebalanced when all excess supplies or demands are eliminated. See Figure 4.2 for a schematic of the rebalancing process.

A simple numerical illustration

I'll use the example input-output table provided in Appendix 4A to analyze a few simple economic shocks. In the simplest shock each sector suffers a proportionate reduction in output. If a disaster eliminates 50 percent of both sectors' capacity, then output in sectors S1 and S2 would be limited to 50 and 75, respectively. The outcome of such a constraint is self-evident. Eventually, shipments to each of the sectors will shrink, as will income to households. They all decline by 50 percent. Household spending for each of the two sectors' products will also shrink by 50 percent. Exports are assumed to shrink proportionately

Figure 4.2 Rebalancing Algorithm

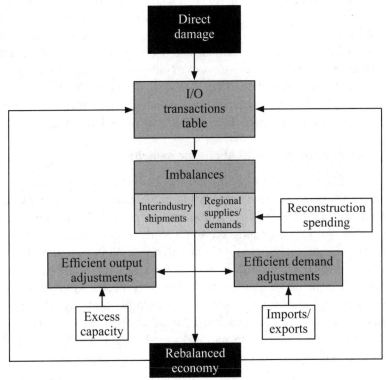

SOURCE: Author's rendition.

as well. The final result is self-evident: the economy will shrink by 50 percent.

This is of course the simplest of cases. Things get a bit more complicated when the pattern of production is limited in some disproportionate way and reconstruction spending amplifies the effects of bottlenecks. In addition, shortages can be avoided through imports or utilizing excess capacity of the region's factories. These are but a few of the options contained in the algorithm.

One last note: the economy can rebalance at many levels. Even in the previous example, balance could have been achieved at 25 percent of predisaster production or even at zero. It is important, therefore, that rebalancing occur in light of some objective. The one that makes the most sense is to rebalance in a way that maximizes the region's post-event income. However, a result that maximizes regional income may not be the one produced by market forces. Since I have called CGE into question (due to unreliable estimates of substitution elasticities, among other problems), I will defend the algorithm's result as the best feasible outcome. This at least provides an envelope of outcomes that policymakers can use to compare different hazards or mitigation strategies.

A few additional notes about the algorithm

The CSU algorithm is based on a 20-sector interindustry table, while rebalancing is achieved by an iterative procedure where sectoral outputs are adjusted within the confines of postevent constraints and capacities. Adjustments proceed until the algorithm finds that all other feasible adjustment patterns yield an inferior level of regional income. The process is repeated each month throughout the period of recovery, yielding a measure of how much the region's income is impacted. Finally, the algorithm tracks shifts in interregional trade as rebalancing alters the region's import-export mix. In addition, it accounts for financial liabilities incurred both nationally and regionally. Liabilities are amortized and household demand is adjusted accordingly. The entire process is complex but has been tested and proved to yield reasonable results. A full discussion of the process is beyond the scope of the chapter, but the outlines of a typical result provide some useful insights into how a stricken economy is likely to rebound.

A Prototypical Pattern of Economic Recovery

Figure 4.3 shows what is typically observed after a disaster. Initially there is some disruption of income flows and a decline in spending. Then, as reconstruction begins and damaged sectors are restored, the economy rebounds until gains are observed. In most instances the rebuilding stimulus produces an economic boom exceeding the predisaster level of activity. Eventually recovery is complete and reconstruction spending dries up. If reconstruction is financed externally (via insurance or federal aid), regional income can be expected to subside to the

Figure 4.3 Prototypical Regional Loss Pattern

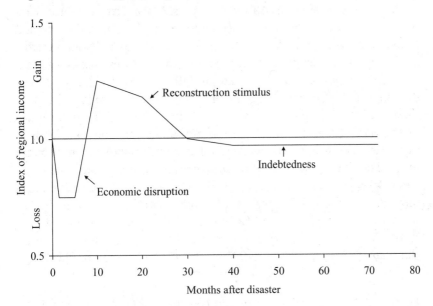

SOURCE: Author's calculations.

pre-event level. If, however, the region is forced to draw upon savings or borrow, the added debt burden acts as a drag on future income, since households and local government are forced to offset the debt by curtailing spending. Total loss is simply the discounted sum of the stream of losses and gains, as shown in Figure 4.3.

The national pattern looks similar. Disruption ripples to surrounding regions via shifts in imports and exports, the use of extraregional construction talent, and the liabilities incurred nationally.

Hurricane Katrina: An Illustration of How the Model Works

Direct damage to the Gulf region as a result of Hurricane Katrina has been estimated at around $200 billion (give or take $50 billion). This seemingly fuzzy estimate is in fact rather precise given that regional and national economic losses have yet to be tabulated. I took this opportunity to exercise the algorithm in order to come up with an estimate of what Katrina cost New Orleans Parish and the country as a whole. As expected, parish income fell sharply after the storm. Disruptions to tourism, oil and gas operations, and barge traffic rippled throughout the region. This decline was partially offset by an immediate injection of spending for relief and recovery. At the same time that New Orleans proper was in a state of collapse, two conflicting forces that impacted the economies of neighboring regions were set in motion. First, the New Orleans economy was so damaged that some of the relief and reconstruction stimulus leaked to surrounding economies. That is to say, outside construction talent and other related imports were brought into the city to supplement what survived the storm. Economies outside New Orleans benefited as a result. Second, as the New Orleans economy shrank, normal imports into the region declined as well. Figure 4.4 shows the results of the CSU simulation. The upper line shows the recovery path for New Orleans proper, while the lower line provides an estimate of the total loss to both New Orleans and the rest of the nation.

Figure 4.4 Economic Loss Inside and Outside New Orleans (Delayed Reconstruction)

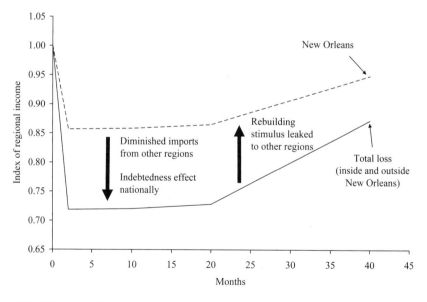

SOURCE: Author's calculations.

Figure 4.5 The Economic Impact of Katrina Contrasted with Andrew

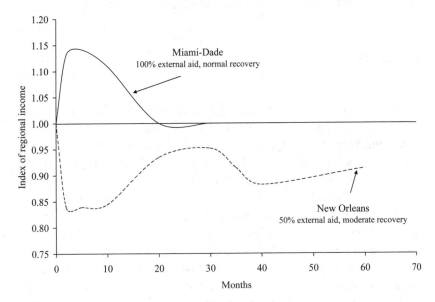

SOURCE: Author's calculations.

One might ask why the New Orleans economy suffered so much. To help answer this question, the economic repercussions of Hurricane Andrew on Miami–Dade County were calculated using the algorithm. Figure 4.5 shows the results. In contrast to Katrina, Andrew produced little long-term impact, a difference attributable to four factors. First, Katrina caused about five times the damage. That alone would explain much of the difference. Second, the New Orleans economy is significantly smaller than the Miami-Dade economy, which could cope with bottlenecks by drawing upon a larger internal excess capacity. Third, since Andrew's winds were the primary cause of damage, property insurance covered most of the loss. Because normal homeowners policies exclude flooding, little of the flood loss (the primary source of damage from Katrina) was insured. Finally, New Orleans faced a housing shortage, so it was difficult to attract outside reconstruction talent. Furthermore, the city became embroiled in a contentious debate concerning how to deal with the ongoing flood hazard. The resulting reconstruction delays still limit the amount of rebuilding that has occurred.

FINAL REMARKS

This chapter has been divided into retrospective and prospective parts. The first part emphasized a few key ideas that, with the aid of hindsight, seem to be logical extensions of water resources economics and the economics of information. Having said that, I am struck by the power of these ideas. I believe that even the simplest of cost-loss models offers valuable insights that are too often lost on policymakers. The confused debate over climate change policy serves to buttress my point. The most puzzling aspect of the literature of the 1960s and 1970s is that so little effort was devoted to categorizing and measuring losses, despite the fact that cost-loss models are worthless without a reasonable loss assessment. Much of this early work was devoted to conceptualizing the problem, where loss was supposed to be self-evident. The second part of the chapter, the prospective view, suggested several topics that need additional attention. Finally, I took a controversial position regarding the use of survey techniques, time series analysis, and CGE. I hold that these methodologies have limited value for predicting how regions are likely to be impacted by unique events. More important, the economic climate has shifted drastically from the time when generous federal aid was available and little excess housing capacity existed. It is dangerous to rely on models that were calibrated using economic conditions that may no longer apply.

Appendix 4A
A Primer on Interindustry Analysis

Input-output tables are the foundation of regional economics. As the name implies, an input-output table traces the flow of products from industry to industry and from industry to households, to government, and for export. It also traces the ingredients inherent in an industry's production (it is, in effect, a recipe). Operational tables can contain as few as 10 sectors or as many as 360. Table 4A.1 shows a simple two-sector table.

The columns represent the shipment of goods from industry to industry, to households, and as exports. The right-hand summation is the total shipped (in the case of each industry), the total income earned (in the case of households) and the total amount imported into the region (in the case of imports). The units shown are typically measured in dollars. So, using the row of the first sector, S1, to illustrate, $20 billion is shipped from the first sector to itself: for example, oil may be used to produce more oil. An additional $45 billion worth is shipped to the second sector, $30 billion to households, and $5 billion exported from the region. The total amount shipped from S1 is therefore $100 billion. The numbers in the first column are interpreted differently. Sector 1's total output is $100 billion (the bottom of column 1). Of this total, Sector 1 contributes $20 billion and Sector 2 contributes $40 billion. Household income in the form of payments for labor and investments amount to another $20 billion of the total, and finally imports of $20 billion from elsewhere make up the remaining part of the total. The shaded area is referred to as interindustry demands. Note that gross shipments must equal supply (gross product) for the economy to be in balance.

Any shock to this economy will begin with a restriction in supply, which then sets a number of adjustments in motion. Declining production means lower income for workers, which reduces household demand for consumer items. Declining production also results in bottlenecks in the production of other interrelated industries. Such restrictions feed back to the sector suffering the initial shock. Although somewhat simple to describe, an operational model requires a complex algorithm, which is briefly described in the main body of the chapter.

Table 4A.1 Example, Input-Output Table: A Typical Interindustry Table

	S1	S2	Households	Exports	Gross shipments
S1	20	45	30	5	100
S2	40	15	30	65	150
Households	20	60	0	0	80
Imports	20	30	20	0	70
Gross product	100	150	80	70	400

NOTE: S1 = industry sector 1; S2 = industry sector 2.

References

Becker, Gary S. 2008. "We're Not Headed for a Depression." *Wall Street Journal,* October 7, A:27. http://online.wsj.com/article/SB122333679431409639 .html (accessed December 7, 2009).

Dacy, D.C., and H. Kunreuther. 1969. *Economics of Natural Disasters: The Implications for Federal Policy.* New York: Free Press.

Emanuel, Kerry. 2005. "Increasing Destructiveness of Tropical Cyclones over the Past 30 Years." *Nature* 436(7051): 686–688.

Hirshleifer, Jack. 1987. *Economic Behavior in Adversity.* Chicago: University of Chicago Press.

Howe, Charles W., and Harold C. Cochrane. 1976. "A Decision Model for Adjusting to Natural Hazard Events with Application to Urban Snow Storms." *Review of Economics and Statistics* 58(1): 50–58.

Lave, Lester B. 1963. "The Value of Better Weather Information to the Raisin Industry." *Econometrica* 31(1–2): 151–164.

Maass, Arthur, Maynard M. Hufschmidt, Robert Dorfman, Harold A. Thomas Jr., Stephan A. Marglin, and Gordon Maskew Fair. 1962. *Design of Water-Resource Systems.* Cambridge, MA: Harvard University Press.

Nelson, Richard R., and Sidney G. Winter. 1964. "A Case Study in the Economics of Information and Coordination: The Weather Forecasting System." *Quarterly Journal of Economics* 78(3): 420–441.

Pielke, R.A. 2005. "Meteorology: Are There Trends in Hurricane Destruction?" *Nature* 438(7071): E11.

Russell, Clifford. 1970. "Losses from Natural Hazards." *Land Economics* 46(4): 383–393.

U.S. Congress. 1966. *A Unified National Program for Managing Flood Losses.* House Task Force on Federal Flood Control Policy. 89th Cong., 2nd sess. H. Doc. 465. Washington, DC: U.S. Government Printing Office.

5
Private Solutions to Public Disasters

Self-Reliance and Social Resilience

Peter J. Boettke
Daniel J. Smith
George Mason University

. . . What has so often excited wonder [is] the great rapidity with which countries recover from a state of devastation; the disappearance, in a short time, of all traces of the mischiefs done by earthquakes, floods, hurricanes, and the ravages of war. An enemy lays waste a country by fire and sword, and destroys or carries away nearly all the moveable wealth existing in it: all the inhabitants are ruined, and yet in a few years after, everything is much as it was before.

—John Stuart Mill (1848)

It is often in the aftermath of the worst calamities of nature and war that the power of human ingenuity and resilience is most clearly demonstrated. John Stuart Mill, writing in 1848, noted that observers were frequently amazed at the rapidity with which inhabitants of a devastated area were able to recover. It is at the very time when public and private infrastructure and formal institutions are at their weakest—following a public disaster—that civil society would be expected to collapse. Yet calamity after calamity has demonstrated the resounding ability of private actors to coordinate recoveries from the most severe of crises.

Unfortunately, not all catastrophes are followed by rapid or even complete recoveries. Slow or incomplete recoveries are attributable in part to the uncontrollable features of the disaster, such as its magnitude or its particular form. Mill argued that large-scale destruction of human capital hinders recovery because local knowledge is essential in coordinating a rapid recovery. A more important factor, especially for economists and policymakers, is the presence of institutional features that can significantly impede the natural tendency of unfettered people to achieve a complete and rapid recovery following a disaster.

Profit-seeking entrepreneurs are vital to any recovery process. Entrepreneurs must be able to unrestrictedly allocate resources to their most urgent employments, as expressed by customers through prices. Any interference with the structure of prices distorts the signals that entrepreneurs receive, misdirecting or hampering their efforts. Misallocation of resources can literally be a matter of life and death in the immediate aftermath of a natural disaster or war. Price ceilings dampen the ability of profits to induce increased supply of needed goods and services, and they distort the ability of prices to signal consumers to ration and economize scarce resources. Poor policy unnecessarily blocks and inhibits the labor and capital adjustments necessary for a complete and timely recovery by distorting entrepreneurial calculation and preventing entrepreneurs from allocating resources to their most productive uses.

Despite the interference of regulations and uncertainty brought about by government action, humankind has demonstrated a remarkable resilience following a natural or man-made disaster. We argue that this is due to the civilizing and coordinating roles played by civil society. For-profit companies, charities, and churches play a vital role in the recovery process. These organizations have proven to be the first and the best-equipped responders to disasters, jump-starting the recovery process.

COMPOUNDING NATURE'S FURY WITH HUMAN FOLLY

Humankind has shown an amazing resilience when it comes to overcoming nature's fury. Yet when nature's fury is compounded with human folly, this resilience may suffer, eroded by corruption, signal distortions, and regime uncertainty. Ironically, it is often well-intentioned people who create the folly that magnifies nature's fury due to a misunderstanding of the way incentives affect human behavior.

We use the case of Hurricane Katrina to show what types of institutions and policies are robust to natural disasters, allowing for maximum speed and totality of recovery. We show how natural disasters can magnify the adverse effects of poor institutions and policies already in place. Hurricane Katrina hit Louisiana in August 2005, causing over $100 billion in property damage and 1,800 deaths (Chamlee-Wright and Rothschild 2007), making it one of the worst natural disasters to ever hit the United States. This destruction has been amplified by policies already in place, such as flood insurance and a corrupt levee board; by policies in the immediate aftermath, such as excessive layers of regulation; and in the long term through the creation of instability and uncertainty for investors.

Even though entrepreneurs were burdened with excessive and inhibiting regulations and poor policy, civil society was still able to show an amazing resilience in the aftermath of Hurricane Katrina. Corporations like Wal-Mart and Home Depot, as well as small businesses like gas stations, were able to respond quickly to the devastation, providing necessary goods and services that would allow more businesses and residents to come back to New Orleans. Profit-seeking entrepreneurs and private charities and churches played a central coordinating role in the aftermath of Katrina.

Pre-Katrina

The Army Corps of Engineers was entrusted with overseeing and constructing levees around Louisiana after the Great Flood of 1927, though the federal government had been overseeing the levees since creating the Mississippi River Commission in 1879 (Davis 2000). The Army Corps of Engineers was caught in conflicting layers of bureaucracy, primarily between the demands and desires of the federal government and the local citizens and politicians of Louisiana.

Three years prior to Katrina, McQuaid and Schleifstein (2002) issued a report concluding that New Orleans's inadequate levees would not withstand a direct hit by a hurricane (Horne 2006). John Barry (1998) wrote a book detailing the history of the Mississippi Flood of 1927, especially focusing on the failures of the Army Corps of Engineers and local politicians to take flood control seriously. John McPhee

(1989) wrote a book detailing how the levees would eventually fail; Eric Berger, a science journalist, reported on the devastation that a direct hit on New Orleans would cause (Berger 2001; Brinkley 2006). Despite such warnings from these and other experts, no substantial measures were taken to fortify the weakened and often ill-constructed levees (van Heerdon and Bryan 2006). When Katrina hit, the Army Corps of Engineers was managing a largely dilapidated system of levees insufficient to stand up to a storm of the magnitude of Katrina. Not only did the levees lack structural integrity, but the construction was also persistently behind schedule: upgrades had been pushed back as long as 13 years, leaving one section of flood work still unfinished when Katrina hit (Horne 2006).

The poor state of the levees was primarily due to the corruption on the levee board.[1] Adamantly and successfully resisting the advice of the Army Corps of Engineers, the levee board fortified frontal protection for the levees instead of focusing on an extensive network of pumps up to several miles inland (Horne 2006). This frontal protection—a system of floodgates—came in at one-third the cost of the favored pump and levee arrangement. However, it required continuous maintenance by the levee board, a task board members were not willing to commit themselves to.

Local politicians were able to funnel federal money earmarked for levee renovation and construction to benefit special-interest groups. The shipping industry successfully lobbied for harbor upgrades and canal dredging projects from this federal money, both projects that actually increased the chances of hurricane damage (Brinkley 2006). In addition, local politicians who controlled the Levee Board and the Sewage and Water Board resisted undertaking costly and unpopular but highly recommended projects in order to bolster voter support by devoting resources to more immediate problems facing New Orleans, such as corruption, schooling, and urban infrastructure problems (Brinkley 2006; Cooper and Block 2006).

With the levees standing 14 feet above the average water level of Lake Pontchartrain, locals believed themselves safe as long as the city pumps were working to take care of any spillovers. This belief, however, was predicated on the assumption that the levees would hold up. Charitable organizations, such as the Red Cross, were aware of the danger that a large storm posed to these insufficient levees and refused to operate within the flood zone. The condition of the levees was bad enough that a significant number of the personnel in charge of managing the levees evacuated prior to the storm, leaving the levees understaffed (Horne 2006). Though the initial break in the levee was only 20 feet and could have been shored up with the heavy equipment and sandbags owned by the levee agency, levee employees did not respond and the break turned into a 200-foot gap.

While local politicians were shirking their duty to maintain the system of levees, state and federal government officials were actively encouraging homeowners and businesses to reside in the disaster-prone areas threatened by the dilapidated levees. Subsidized flood insurance and the expectation of postdisaster relief brought about what economists call moral hazard problems in disaster-prone areas. Moral hazard problems occur when people are protected from incurring the full cost of their choices and thus make worse and more costly decisions than they would absent such protection. Lowering the cost of residing in areas with high flood and wind risk artificially increases the number of people and the amount of property in disaster-prone areas (Sutter 2008). In an unmolested market, increased insurance rates and the expectation of incurring storm damages would force residents to account for and bear the cost of living in disaster-prone areas.

Furthermore, state governments have been notoriously resistant to letting insurance companies mandate mitigation efforts by customers in these high-risk areas. When cost-effective preventive measures are necessary in order to obtain insurance, an incentive exists to build more structurally sound buildings. Even such simple measures as installing window shutters can significantly reduce the probability of wind damage.

State governments interfere with insurance companies' risk assessments and premiums for various types of mitigation in two ways. First, several states in disaster-prone areas require state approval of mitigation discounts, allowing competing insurance companies and politically motivated elected officials to second-guess insurance companies' decisions. Second, some states, such as Louisiana, Florida, and North Carolina, require discounts for certain mitigation practices. Since insurance companies already have the incentives to offer discounts for effective mitigation practices, government interference, when binding, requires allocation of resources to mitigation measures that have not been proven effective. Laws that require insurance companies to fund sham mitigation practices stem from political favors both to interested parties and to genuinely concerned politicians who do not have a full understanding of insurance markets.

New Orleans's long tradition of special-interest legislation, in addition to leading to poor levee maintenance and construction, also shackled entrepreneurs' abilities to respond to consumers' needs in the wake of the havoc created by Katrina. In postdisaster recoveries, such restrictions prove extraordinarily burdensome for two primary reasons. First, the bureaucratic process of applying for permits, inspections, and assistance is especially difficult when many public buildings are damaged and public employees displaced. Filling out the paperwork required for engaging in various forms of business activities is a daunting process even when public infrastructure is not shut down or understaffed. Second, as John Stuart Mill pointed out, the return of people with local human capital is essential to the recovery process. Entrepreneurs, vital for recovery, may become frustrated by a complicated bureaucratic process and may simply choose to not return following a disaster. At best, regulatory processes only slow down and prevent entrepreneurs from putting their human capital to immediate use. In order to attract residents and other business owners back to the affected areas, an initial set of enterprising business owners must return and provide basic goods and services. Residents and other business owners waiting for these basic goods and services to be available before returning are, over time, more likely to establish themselves in the cities they took refuge in, making it costlier to return.

Occupational licensing, granted to construction unions to artificially increase wages, restricted construction experts from other states from setting up shop in the disaster-stricken areas to jump-start the rebuilding process. The six-month waiting period mandated for a construction permit was not rescinded in the wake of the damage created by Katrina. To its credit, the city of New Orleans did suspend inspections on construction projects, allowing, for instance, carpenters and electricians to inspect their own work. Historic preservation regulations also inhibited rebuilding in New Orleans. Draconian preservation laws were applied in historic districts, making it difficult for contractors to quickly rebuild and restore historic buildings affected by severe flooding. Preexisting restrictions on the adult-to-child ratio for child care centers were also not relaxed following the storm (Chamlee-Wright 2008a). To initiate progress toward recovery, entrepreneurs and business owners needed places offering care and supervision for their children. Even two years after Katrina hit, only 94 of 275 day care centers in New Orleans had reopened. With so many damaged buildings and missing employees, the adult-to-child capacity restrictions meant that many parents were unable to focus completely on recovery efforts. The numerous residents who fled with their children to cities such as Houston and Atlanta found it hard to take on full-time employment due to similar restrictions in those cities.

Zoning regulations and building codes also shackled entrepreneurs in their efforts to speedily reopen stores to offer basic services and goods. The opening of a health clinic was delayed by nearly six months because it was located in a residential zone and had building code violations such as a handicap ramp with hand rails on only one side. Similarly, a laundry had to wait weeks for an inspection after the building was completed and ready to open up.

Layers of regulation and profit windfalls from postdisaster relief create an institutional environment ripe for corruption. In 2004, Louisiana was ranked fortieth out of 50 states in the Pacific Research Institute's Economic Freedom of the States Index (Huang, McCormick, and McQuillan 2004) and had relatively high costs of conducting business compared to other states. In addition, Louisiana was ranked the third most corrupt state in the nation in 2004 (Corporate Crime Reporter 2004).

During Katrina

The folly already in place prior to Katrina, which drastically increased the amount of damage the storm caused, was also compounded with folly during the storm and its immediate aftermath. While most economists are familiar with the concept of the tragedy of the commons, a term coined by the biologist Garrett Hardin, most are not familiar with the tragedy of the anticommons. The tragedy of the anticommons occurs when several government agencies have the ability to regulate and control a common area, creating unnecessary, and often repetitive and even conflicting, layers of bureaucracy. Additional layers of bureaucracy, especially following a disaster, can cost lives by slowing down the response times of entrepreneurs. In addition, complicated layers of bureaucracy, especially when combined with political windfalls from disaster relief, drastically increase the chances of venality.

The relief efforts for Hurricane Katrina orchestrated by FEMA have been notoriously plagued by corruption and abuse. In fact, according to the Government Accountability Office, the cost of corruption and abuse for Hurricanes Katrina and Rita could reach $1.4 billion (Kutz and Ryan 2006). In a study on natural disasters and corruption, Leeson and Sobel (2008) found that every additional $1 per capita spent on disaster relief by FEMA increases corruption in the average state by up to 2.5 percent, due to the windfalls created by the programs. This suggests that the states along the Gulf Coast might be notoriously corrupt precisely because they are frequently hit by natural disasters. Leeson and Sobel estimate that eliminating FEMA disaster relief would reduce corruption by more than 20 percent in the average state. In a separate article, Leeson and Sobel (2007) trace the origins of the corruption to the time-sensitive nature of disaster relief; increased oversight shows little promise in curbing this corruption because, in their words, "protocol will take a backseat when disasters actually strike."

When infrastructure and normal modes of communicating and organizing activity are slow, incomplete, and impeded by interference following a public disaster, the need to allow market prices to adjust to communicate information to the relevant actors becomes even more important. Hayek (1945) discusses the heavily dispersed nature of knowledge and the importance of a freely fluctuating price system as the most efficient system to coordinate economic activity across an array of activities because of its ability to convey the specific knowledge of time and place to the relevant economic actors. With so many needs after a natural disaster, it is difficult, especially for an altruistic government agent operating in the field, to decide whose and what needs should be met first. Sobel and Leeson (2007) find that while private actors are able to respond to transient, decentralized information in a timely manner following a disaster, public officials are forced to make decisions with, at best, scanty and outdated information.

Price controls following a disaster are known for distorting price signals, which is counterproductive at a time when those signals are most needed to coordinate the allocation of resources to their most urgent employment. William Carden (2009) noted that emergency situations are inherently chaotic and that a well-functioning unmolested price system can significantly reduce the chaos. Price ceilings discourage economical consumption and take away the profit-seeking motive for entrepreneurs to find innovative ways of allocating resources where the demand is highest.

Post-Katrina

Continuous government interference in the market, policy reversals, and varying responses to disasters create uncertainty for market actors. This uncertainty may inhibit entrepreneurial investment in current profit opportunities. Robert Higgs (1997) calls this process in which government adversely affects investment by not credibly adhering to a set policy *regime uncertainty*. In the aftermath of a disaster, the stymieing effect of regime uncertainty on investment is magnified, as it paralyzes the entrepreneurship and investment necessary for a full and rapid recovery. Market actors, left in the dark concerning the nature and timing of goods and services to be provided by government agencies, cut back on much-needed investment. Government regulations, such as price controls, distort the signaling process and prevent the market adjustment that is at the very heart of economic efficiency.

By focusing on standard postdisaster recovery procedures, public officials disregarded the necessary role of private actors in the recovery process (Chamlee-Wright and Storr 2008a). Focusing on procuring more federal dollars, imposing stronger regulations, and periodically implementing new recovery plans, policymakers intruded on the recovery process, preventing entrepreneurs from rapidly returning to their businesses. In a structured set of neutral interviews, residents named barriers erected by government policies and programs, in particular those intended to assist redevelopment, as the biggest challenge they had faced since returning (Chamlee-Wright and Storr 2007).

Despite these needless barriers, entrepreneurs exercised persistence and creativity to coordinate the start of a recovery. Population estimates for the New Orleans MSA show that its total population reached 86 percent of pre-Katrina levels by July of 2008 (GNOCDC 2008), as shown in Table 5.1.[2] Although the area remains far short of a full recovery, especially in the parishes most severely hit by Katrina, the data nonetheless reflects an impressive display of resiliency. This resilience, however, is largely due to private-sector responses, and not formulaic public-sector responses (Boettke et al. 2007). In fact, those areas where public-sector influence undermined private-sector response times show the least recovery progress.

SELF-RELIANCE AND SOCIAL RESILIENCE

According to Nobel Laureate Thomas Schelling, the primary problem residents of New Orleans faced in the recovery process was that of coordinating expectations (Gosselin 2005). If residents expected people to come back and work to bring about a recovery, then they would. On the other hand, if residents did not expect others to come back, they in fact would not come back, and the human capital necessary for recovery would never materialize. Private corporations, such as Wal-Mart and Home Depot, and determined small business owners were able to solve Schelling's coordination problem by being the first movers. By quickly getting their stores reopened and their employees back in town, these businesses were able to provide the basic goods and services that were necessary for other residents and business owners to come back to New Orleans as well.

Through in-depth interviews she conducted in New Orleans, Emily Chamlee-Wright (2007; 2008b) found that private actors played a large role in coordinating a recovery through mutual assistance, commercial cooperation, and private reestablishment of community resources. Residents with house damage and business owners who found their stores damaged or looted would not have been able to return immediately after Katrina to jump-start the recovery process without mutual assistance. Returning residents were able to coordinate a return with

Table 5.1 Population by Parish, New Orleans (LA) MSA

	Jefferson	Orleans	Plaquemines	St. Bernard	St. Charles	St. John	St. Tammany	Total
July 2005	450,848	455,046	28,565	64,890	50,116	45,568	217,367	1,312,400
July 2006	422,222	210,768	21,610	13,924	51,868	47,647	223,863	991,902
July 2007	440,339	288,113	21,597	33,439	51,892	47,678	226,263	1,109,411
July 2008	436,181	311,853	21,276	37,722	51,547	46,994	228,456	1,134,029

SOURCE: GNOCDC (2008).

others by committing to exchanging their different skills and remaining resources. A lumber store owner was able to trade room in his largely undamaged house for assistance in rebuilding his store, which had been badly damaged and looted. Chamlee-Wright also found that commercial entities showed novel and extensive cooperation with each other in order to signal to evacuees that New Orleans would recover and that basic goods and services would be available to returning residents looking to start the recovery process. Companies were willing to offer harder-hit companies generous terms of credit and even free supplies in order to help these other businesses open up to attract more residents back. Churches, such as the Mary Queen of Vietnam Catholic Church, were able to reestablish community services vital for attracting back the local knowledge necessary for a complete and timely recovery.

The Doux-Commerce Thesis, put forth by the Scottish Enlightenment thinkers, holds that commerce plays a key role in civil society: it is the very act of trading that civilizes a society. Through the process of exchange we find mutually beneficial margins that encourage cooperation, and seeking to establish an honest reputation to facilitate future transactions gives business owners and their customers a motive to exhibit desirable moral traits. In the chaotic aftermath of a disaster like Katrina, this civilizing role of reestablishing commerce is necessary for the recovery process.

Although hindered by policies that exacerbated the toll of Katrina, private companies and organizations undertook efforts that significantly eased the severity of the disaster. Horwitz (2009) found that big-box retailers, such as Wal-Mart and Home Depot, operating under the knowledge-generating and incentive-inducing influences of competition, were able to respond significantly faster than FEMA. The private companies managed to get supplies to where they were needed almost directly following the storm. Before Hurricane Katrina even made landfall, both chains had preemptively placed trucks, drivers, and supplies at strategic staging points, out of danger but close enough to rush in supplies right after the storm passed. Wal-Mart, using its efficient supply chain, was able to get all but 15 of 89 damaged stores up and running within 10 days, supplying needed items to Katrina survivors. Within the first three weeks after the storm hit, Wal-Mart delivered almost 2,500 truckloads of supplies to the affected areas, while Home Depot delivered over 800 truckloads. Both organizations left local store managers with discretion so they could respond to local emergency situations. Several Wal-Mart managers were commended for providing free supplies to devastated survivors of the storm.

Churches and private charity organizations also played an important role in the recovery process following Hurricane Katrina. Chamlee-Wright and Storr (2008b, 2009) do an in-depth cultural analysis of a Vietnamese-American community in New Orleans East, finding that the Mary Queen of Vietnam Catholic Church played a central role in the revival of the neighborhood surrounding the church. One of the most surprising features of their study is that the church is located in one of the most damaged areas of New Orleans, one that the Urban Land Institute claimed had little chance of recovery. Within a few weeks after the storm, parishioners were returning and taking the initial steps towards recovery. An astounding 90 percent of the residents around the church had returned by summer 2007, and 70 of the 75 Vietnamese-owned area businesses were up and running. Even compared to less-damaged areas, this was a remarkable recovery.

CONCLUSION

The destruction and upheaval caused by nature's fury are often staggering. Throughout history, unfettered people have been able to overcome the worst tragedies of nature and war, displaying the amazing resilience and ingenuity of humankind. However, when governments impede the very process that allows the rapidity and completeness of recovery, civil society must overcome human folly as well as nature's fury. Placing additional regulatory obstacles and destabilizing programs in the way of entrepreneurs severely compromises the ability of private actors to coordinate a complete and rapid recovery.

It was civil society that forged the way in coordinating a post-Katrina recovery. Entrepreneurs were able to overcome the obstacles created by the hurricane itself and by problematic government regulation in order to provide the basic goods and services necessary to jump-start the recovery process. It was the initial commitments undertaken by businesses and private organizations, as well as the civilizing influence of the reestablishment of commerce, that attracted residents back to New Orleans, demonstrating, once again, the amazing resilience of civil society in overcoming nature's fury.

Notes

1. This corruption persisted even after Katrina hit, when the levee board president used the tragedy of Katrina to hand out lucrative contracts to family members, including his wife's cousin and her son, and even cut himself a check that was $98,000 above the normal stipend (Horne 2006).
2. The parishes of Jefferson, Orleans, and Plaquemines dispute the 2008 figures, claiming that the U.S. Census Bureau has understated these numbers (GNOCDC 2008). If undisputed 2007 figures are used instead of the 2008 figures, then the total population of the New Orleans MSA had reached 85 percent of pre-Katrina levels by July 2007.

References

Barry, John M. 1998. *Rising Tide: The Great Mississippi Flood of 1927 and How It Changed America.* New York: Touchstone.

Berger, Eric. 2001. "Keeping Its Head above Water: New Orleans Faces Doomsday Scenario." *Houston Chronicle*, December 1, A:29.

Boettke, Peter, Emily Chamlee-Wright, Peter Gordon, Sanford Ikeda, Peter Leeson, and Russell Sobel. 2007. "The Political, Economic, and Social Aspects of Katrina." *Southern Economic Journal* 74(2): 363–376.

Brinkley, Douglas. 2006. *The Great Deluge: Hurricane Katrina, New Orleans, and the Mississippi Gulf Coast.* New York: HarperCollins.

Carden, William. 2009. "Sound and Fury: Rhetoric and Rebound after Katrina." *Journal of Business Valuation and Economic Loss Analysis* 4(2): Article 2.

Chamlee-Wright, Emily. 2007. "The Long Road Back: Signal Noise in the Post-Katrina Context." *Independent Review* 12(2): 235–259.

———. 2008a. *The Entrepreneur's Role in Post-Disaster Recovery: Implications for Post-Disaster Recovery Policy.* Mercatus Policy Series, Policy Primer 6. Arlington, VA: Mercatus Center at George Mason University.

———. 2008b. "Signaling Effects of Commercial and Civil Society in Post-Katrina Reconstruction." *International Journal of Social Economics* 35(7/8): 615–626.

Chamlee-Wright, Emily, and Daniel Rothschild. 2007. *Disastrous Uncertainty: How Government Disaster Policy Undermines Community Rebound.* Mercatus Policy Series, Policy Comment 9. Arlington, VA: Mercatus Center at George Mason University.

Chamlee-Wright, Emily, and Virgil Storr. 2007. "Community Resilience in New Orleans East: Deploying the Cultural Toolkit within a Vietnamese-American Community." Mercatus working paper. Arlington, VA: Mercatus Center at George Mason University.

———. 2008a. *The Entrepreneur's Role in Post-Disaster Community Recovery: Implications for Post-Disaster Recovery Policy.* Mercatus Policy Series, Policy Primer 6. Arlington, VA: Mercatus Center at George Mason University.

———. 2008b. "The Political Economy of Post-Katrina Recovery: Public Choice Style Critiques from the Ninth Ward, New Orleans." Mercatus working paper. Arlington, VA: Mercatus Center at George Mason University.

———. 2009. "Club Goods and Post-Disaster Community Return." *Rationality and Society* 21(4): 429–458.

Cooper, Christopher, and Robert Block. 2006. *Disaster: Hurricane Katrina and the Failure of Homeland Security.* New York: Times Books.

Corporate Crime Reporter. 2004. *Public Corruption in the United States.* Washington, DC: National Press Club. http://www.corporatecrimereporter.com/corruptreport.pdf (accessed November 11, 2009).

Davis, Donald W. 2000. "Historical Perspective on Crevasses, Levees, and the Mississippi River." In *Transforming New Orleans and Its Environs: Centuries of Change,* Craig E. Colten, ed. Pittsburgh: University of Pittsburgh Press, pp. 84–106.

Gosselin, Peter. 2005. "On Their Own in Battered New Orleans." *Los Angeles Times,* December 4. http://articles.latimes.com/2005/dec/04/nation/na-orleansrisk4 (accessed November 6, 2009).

Greater New Orleans Community Data Center (GNOCDC). 2008. *Census Population Estimates 2000–2008 for New Orleans MSA.* http://www.gnocdc.org/census_pop_estimates.html (accessed March 11, 2010).

Hayek, Friedrich. 1945. "The Use of Knowledge in Society." *American Economic Review* 35(4): 519–530.

Higgs, Robert. 1997. "Regime Uncertainty: Why the Great Depression Lasted So Long and Why Prosperity Resumed after the War." *The Independent Review* 1(4): 561–590.

Horne, Jed. 2006. *Breach of Faith: Hurricane Katrina and the Near Death of a Great American City.* New York: Random House.

Horwitz, Steven. 2009. "Wal-Mart to the Rescue: Private Enterprise's Response to Hurricane Katrina." *Independent Review* 13(4): 511–528.

Huang, Y., Robert McCormick, and Lawrence McQuillan. 2004. *U.S. Economic Freedom Index: 2004 Report*. San Francisco: Pacific Research Institute.

Kutz, Gregory D., and John J. Ryan. 2006. "Hurricanes Katrina and Rita Disaster Relief: Improper and Potentially Fraudulent Individual Assistance Payments Estimated to Be between $600 Million and $1.4 Billion." Washington, DC: U.S. Congress. Committee on Homeland Security. House Subcommittee on Investigations. Testimony, 106th Cong., 2d sess., pp. 1–26. http://www.gao.gov/new.items/d06844t.pdf (accessed November 11, 2009).

Leeson, Peter, and Russell Sobel. 2007. *The Impact of FEMA on U.S. Corruption: Implications for Policy*. Mercatus Policy Series, Policy Comment 8. Arlington, VA: Mercatus Center at George Mason University.

———. 2008. "Weathering Corruption." *Journal of Law and Economics* 51(4): 667–681.

McPhee, John. 1989. *The Control of Nature*. New York: Farrar, Straus, and Giroux.

McQuaid, John, and Mark Schleifstein. 2002. "Washing Away." *New Orleans Times-Picayune*, June. 23–27. http://www.nola.com/hurricane/content.ssf?/washingaway/index.html (accessed December 7, 2009).

Mill, John Stuart. 1848. *Principles of Political Economy*. New York: Augustus M. Kelley.

Sobel, Russell, and Peter Leeson. 2007. "The Use of Knowledge in Natural-Disaster Relief Management." *Independent Review* 11(4): 519–532.

Sutter, Daniel. 2008. *Building a Safe Port in the Storm: Private vs. Public Choices in Hurricane Mitigation*. Mercatus Policy Series, Policy Comment 21. Arlington, VA: Mercatus Center at George Mason University.

van Heerdon, Ivor, and Mike Bryan. 2006. *The Storm: What Went Wrong and Why During Hurricane Katrina—The Inside Story from One Louisiana Scientist*. New York: Penguin.

6
The Socioeconomic
Impact of Tornadoes

Daniel Sutter
University of Texas–Pan American

Kevin M. Simmons
Austin College

Tornadoes are nature's most powerful and destructive storms, capable of producing winds in excess of 300 miles per hour, yet they are notoriously capricious, leveling one home and leaving the next undamaged. The United States experiences more than 1,200 tornadoes per year, and since 1900 over 15,000 lives have been lost in tornadoes. The deadliest tornado in U.S. history, the 1925 Tri-State Tornado, tracked across three states and killed 695 persons, devastating entire towns. Tornadoes have occupied a place in the national consciousness at least since the 1939 movie *The Wizard of Oz*, when a Kansas twister blew Dorothy and Toto to Oz. Every spring thousands of people spend weeks trekking across the Plains chasing tornadoes.

How can economists or social scientists contribute to our knowledge of tornadoes? While cloud dynamics and the technical properties of weather radars are outside these fields, economics can help us understand the impact of tornadoes on society. Economics can provide relevant evidence on several issues related to societal impacts:

- Have tornadoes become less deadly over time?

- If so, how much have the efforts of the National Weather Service (NWS) contributed to this?

- What measures offer the greatest potential to reduce casualties in a cost-effective manner?

An understanding of the causes is necessary to reduce the impacts of severe weather. Just as physicians must understand the causes of illness to successfully treat patients, meteorologists require information about societal impacts. Attempts to reduce casualties not founded on solid analysis could prove unsuccessful or incur excessive costs.

Tornadoes also provide evidence on some questions of significance to policymakers:

• People sometimes have difficulty making sense of small risks of death and either overestimate or underestimate these risks (Camerer and Kunreuther 1989; McClelland, Schulze, and Coursey 1993). Is misperception of risk a problem with tornadoes?

• Can an economic model of information help us understand peoples' reactions to hazard warnings?

• How prevalent is underpreparation for natural hazards? Hurricane Katrina has raised the issue of poor societal preparation for hazards to high salience for policy (Meyer 2006).

Because of the broad reach of tornadoes (they have occurred in all states), their impacts depend on the preparations and actions of essentially all Americans, a fact that underscores the importance of evidence regarding these events.

This chapter analyzes the impact of tornadoes on the United States and is organized as follows. The next section reviews the aggregate impact of tornadoes on the nation, including three main components: 1) the cost of casualties, 2) the value of property damaged or destroyed, and 3) the cost of responding to tornado warnings. Overall the monetized cost of tornadoes is $4.6 billion per year. We then discuss findings on the determinants of tornado casualties, and we use these findings to analyze how the impacts might be reduced. The final section offers a brief conclusion.

THE SOCIETAL COST OF TORNADOES

Tornadoes threaten life and limb, and they damage and destroy property. Tornado warnings are also costly, because people must disrupt their daily activities to take shelter during a tornado warning. To provide perspective on the impact of tornadoes, we monetize the value of casualties, damages, and sheltering costs, based on U.S. averages for 1996–2006. Damage is the easiest to monetize, and we use inflation-adjusted property damage as reported by the NWS, which averaged $1.07 billion annually (in 2007 dollars).[1] Note that 1996–2006 included the tornado with the greatest reported damage in U.S. history, the May 3, 1999, Oklahoma City F5 tornado.[2]

A total of 645 tornado fatalities occurred between 1996 and 2006, or 58.6 per year. Comparing fatalities with damage requires application of a dollar figure for the lives lost. The value of a statistical life as revealed in market trade-offs constitutes a reasonable way to value lives for such public policy purposes.[3] We use the value of a statistical life applied by the Environmental Protection Agency in a benefit-cost analysis of the Clean Air Act (EPA 1997). The EPA used a figure of $4.8 million in 1990 dollars, based on a meta-analysis of dozens of published studies. Adjusting this value for inflation yields a value of $7.6 million in 2007 dollars. The monetized value of tornado fatalities is thus $445 million per year.

Tornadoes injured an average of 999 persons annually. Values of statistical injuries have been developed using market data, and the EPA (1997) has applied monetary values for a variety of injuries. A difficulty arises in applying existing values to tornado injuries due to a dearth of information on the distribution of the severity of tornado injuries. Epidemiological studies in the aftermath of selected tornadoes provide some evidence on the severity of injuries, which overall are not very severe. Brown et al. (2002), for example, found that 76 percent of injuries in the May 3, 1999, Oklahoma tornado outbreak did not require hospitalization and that the average hospital stay was seven days. Carter, Millson, and Allen (1989) found that 83 percent of injuries in the May 31, 1985, Ontario, Canada, tornado outbreak were minor, with an average hospital stay of 12.5 days. Given this evidence, we follow Merrell, Simmons, and Sutter (2005) and use a value of a statistical injury equal to 1 percent of the value of a statistical life, or $76,000. The monetary value of injuries is then $76 million per year.

We turn next to the cost of tornado warnings, that is, the value of time spent under warnings. Although taking cover during a tornado warning can save lives, the disruption of business or leisure activities is costly. Between 1996 and 2004, the NWS issued around 3,500 warnings per year, which were in effect for an average of 41 minutes each.[4] We use the U.S. Census estimated population of the warned county and the duration of each warning to estimate person-hours spent under warnings. The average warned county had a population of 98,000, so an average of 234 million person-hours were spent under warnings annually. For members of the workforce, the hourly wage measures the opportunity cost of time. We use the average civilian nonfarm hourly wage of $17.42 in 2007 (BLS 2007) to value employed persons' time lost, and we value the time of individuals who are not employed, 52 percent of the population, at half this amount. The weighted average value of time is $12.89, and the annual value of time spent under warnings is $3.02 billion.

Table 6.1 summarizes the impacts of tornadoes quantified here. The cost is $4.6 billion per year, and the value of time spent under warnings accounts for nearly two-thirds of this total, property damage 23 percent, fatalities at just under 10 percent, and injuries less than 2 percent. Note that this total does not include societal impacts, such as business interruption, alternative living expenses, and external, community-wide impacts. Although tornado impacts on a metropolitan area are modest, major tornadoes can significantly impact small communities. In April 2007, a tornado heavily damaged the business district of Tulia, Texas (population 4,700). The town's only grocery store never reopened after the tornado, leaving residents with a 60-mile round trip drive to Amarillo for grocery shopping (Martinez and Ewing 2008).

Readers might find the large contribution of time under warnings to the total impact of tornadoes surprising. One way to put the costs of warnings in perspective is to consider how the cost of tornadoes would have differed in the 1920s. Brooks and Doswell (2002) estimate that the U.S. tornado fatality rate fell from 1.8 per million residents then to 0.11 per million in 2000. If the higher 1920s rate occurred today, the nation would experience an average of 960 fatalities per year, not the 59 actually observed since 1996. Applying the $7.6 million value of a statistical life yields a cost of fatalities of $7.3 billion annually; the NWS did not issue warnings in the 1920s, so there is no basis for comparing cost of time spent under warnings. The lethality of tornadoes has

Table 6.1 Annual Impact of Tornadoes

Impact	Amount	Monetized value ($ millions)	% of monetized impact
Property damage	—	1,070	23.2
Fatalities	58.6	445	9.7
Injuries	999	76	1.6
Time under warnings	234 million person-hours	3,020	65.5
Total		4,610	100.0

NOTE: Damage and casualties are averages for 1996–2006, time under warnings an average for 1996–2004. The valuation of lives lost, injuries, and time under warnings is discussed in the text.
SOURCE: National Oceanic and Atmospheric Administration's (NOAA) tornado fatality location data, available from the NOAA by permission.

been so greatly reduced that responding to warnings now represents the largest part of the cost of tornadoes. The total cost is substantially lower today because tornadoes are less deadly.

WHAT ARE THE DETERMINANTS OF TORNADO CASUALTIES?

An analysis of tornado casualties reveals several significant patterns discussed in this section. The figures cited are from a regression analysis of tornado fatalities and injuries from 1986 to 2004. The data set has been constructed by the authors using the Storm Prediction Center's (SPC) national tornado archive, the NWS's tornado warning verification records, and U.S. Census data.[5] The unit of observation is the state tornado segment, because the SPC archive reports separate entries for multistate tornadoes. For simplicity we will usually just say tornadoes and not state tornado segments in the text. Appendix 6A discusses the details of the regression model and precise variable definitions, and Table 6A.1 reports the full results.

Most Tornadoes Are Not Killers

Only 347 of the almost 21,000 tornadoes in our data set resulted in one or more fatalities, and 1,988 resulted in one or more injuries. That is, 98 percent of tornadoes had no fatalities, and 91 percent caused no injuries. The risk to life and limb posed by tornadoes is quite concentrated in powerful storms. The most powerful tornadoes are rated F4 or F5 on the Fujita scale of tornado damage.[6] Nine of the ten F5 tornadoes and 42 percent of F4 tornadoes between 1986 and 2004 killed at least one person, and these tornadoes accounted for 43 percent of fatalities. The 41 tornadoes that resulted in five or more fatalities (less than 0.2 percent of the total) accounted for half of all fatalities.

Tornadoes rated F3 or stronger are much more likely to result in fatalities or injuries. Table 6.2, constructed from the regression analysis, reports fatalities and injuries by tornadoes of different F-scale ratings relative to an F0 tornado. Expected fatalities are about 27,000 times more likely with an F5 tornado than with an F0, and injuries are almost 2,000 times more likely in F5 tornadoes. Both fatalities and injuries increase fairly consistently with each F-scale category increase.

Location, Location, Location

Many observers have noted the vulnerability of mobile homes to tornadoes (American Meteorological Society 1997; Brooks and Doswell 2002; Golden and Adams 2000; Golden and Snow 1991). Figure 6.1 reports tornado fatalities by location as tracked by the NWS for the years

Table 6.2 Tornado Casualties by Fujita Scale Rating

F-scale category	Fatalities	Injuries
F1	15	11
F2	105	65
F3	545	178
F4	2,644	692
F5	26,630	1,808

NOTE: The values in the table are the ratio of expected fatalities or injuries in a tornado of each F-scale category rating relative to an otherwise equivalent F0 tornado.
SOURCE: Authors' calculations.

Figure 6.1   Tornado Fatalities by Location (%)

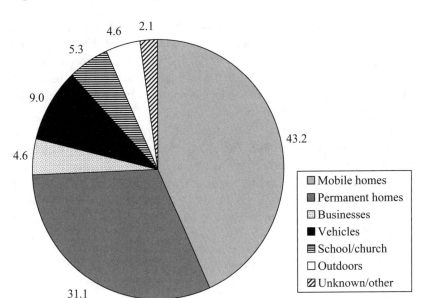

SOURCE: Authors' calculations from NOAA tornado fatality location data.

1985–2007.[7] More fatalities occurred in mobile homes (43 percent) than any other location. Permanent homes, which include single-family homes and apartments, rank second at 31 percent, followed by vehicles at 9 percent, schools and churches, businesses, and outdoor or other locations at about 5 percent each. The proportion of fatalities in manufactured homes is disproportionately high. These structures constituted only 7.6 percent of U.S. housing units in 2000 (U.S. Census Bureau 2000), but the fatality rate for manufactured homes is at least ten times that of permanent homes. Regression analysis confirms the dependence of casualties on the housing stock. An increase of one standard deviation in mobile homes as a proportion of county housing units increases expected fatalities by 36 percent and expected injuries by 26 percent.

Timing Matters

Timing significantly affects casualties, including time of day, day of the week, and month of the year. Tornadoes during the evening and overnight hours are significantly more likely to kill or injure people. Figure 6.2 reports an index for casualties by time of day based on the regression analysis. We divide the day into five time periods, the overnight hours (midnight to 6 a.m.), morning (6 a.m. to noon), early afternoon (noon to 4 p.m.), late afternoon (4 p.m. to 8 p.m.), and late evening (8 p.m. to midnight). The index sets fatalities and injuries from an early afternoon tornado equal to 100, and represents casualties from tornadoes at other times relative to an early afternoon tornado. Fatalities for overnight tornadoes exceed those of early afternoon tornadoes by a factor of nearly 2.5 and those for late evening tornadoes by a factor of

Figure 6.2 Time of Day and Tornado Casualties

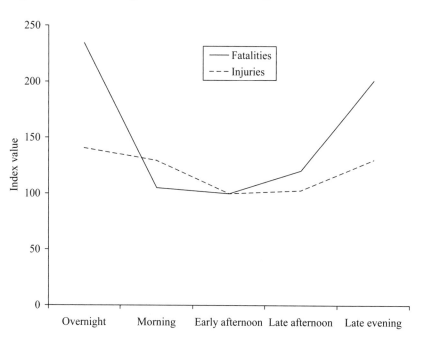

SOURCE: Authors' calculations from the NWS Storm Prediction Center's tornado archive.

more than 2. A similar pattern is observed for injuries, but the amplitude of the time of day effects are not as great; injuries are 43 percent and 32 percent higher overnight and in the late evening, respectively, than for a comparable early afternoon tornado.

Tornado casualties also vary widely by month. Figure 6.3 presents an index of fatalities and injuries by month derived from the regression analysis. The index equals 100 for both fatalities and injuries in February, the month with the deadliest tornadoes. The difference in lethality across months is quite substantial, as a tornado in February yields more than 14 times the fatalities of an otherwise equal tornado in July. Tornadoes are less deadly in the spring and summer months (with the exception of August) than tornadoes in the late fall or winter. Injuries exhibit the same basic pattern, except that again the variation is substantially less than for fatalities (injuries in January tornadoes exceed those in May tornadoes by a factor of 2.5). The low casualty rates

Figure 6.3 Tornado Casualties by Month

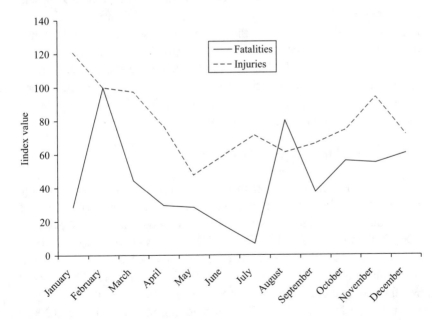

SOURCE: Authors' calculations from the NWS Storm Prediction Center's tornado archive.

in May, June, and July benefit the nation, since these months have the largest numbers of tornadoes, while the high lethality in November, December, January, and February applies to relatively few tornadoes. Although a difference in intensity of storms not fully captured by the F-scale variables may be thought to drive the result, the strongest tornadoes occur in the spring months. Hours of darkness might explain some of the variation over months, because tornadoes that occur after dark are more dangerous (see Ashley, Knmenec, and Schwantes 2008, who control for the exact time of sunset). But variation in casualties across months is much greater than the variation across the day, so darkness probably cannot explain much of the variation over the year. Surprise might drive this result; residents may not expect tornadoes during the winter, and thus are not alert for and ready to respond to a warning. In contrast, during the spring residents might suspect that an ominous thunderstorm could produce a tornado. Surprise would need to affect warning responses, since the regressions control for tornado warnings.

The day of the week also affects fatalities. Intuition suggests that casualties might be higher on either weekends or weekdays. On weekends people might be busy with recreation and leisure activities and not closely following the weather and weather warnings, while weekday tornadoes could occur during evening rush hour traffic jams. The regression analysis finds that weekend tornadoes are more dangerous: expected fatalities and injuries are 40 percent and 8 percent higher, respectively, than for tornadoes during the week, although only the fatalities result attains statistical significance.

The Efforts of the National Weather Service

Protecting persons is part of the mission of the NWS, and tornado warnings have been issued since the 1950s to try to reduce casualties (Doswell, Moller, and Brooks 1999). The NWS installed WSR-88D (Doppler) radars at Weather Forecast Offices (WFOs) across the country between 1992 and 1997. The radars, adapted from military use, allow much better resolution of wind fields in severe storms. Viewers of weather coverage on television are probably familiar with the Doppler radar image of the "hook echo" of a tornado. Simmons and Sutter (2005) analyzed the effect of Doppler radar on tornado warnings and casualties by using the radar installation date for each WFO to determine which tornadoes occurred after installation of the new radars. Over the period from 1986 to 1999, Doppler radar increased the percentage of storms warned for from 35 to 60 percent and the mean lead time from 5.3 to 9.5 minutes; it also reduced the percentage of false alarm warnings from 79 to 76 percent. The new radars also reduced expected fatalities by 45 percent and expected injuries by 40 percent. We update the casualties analysis with these regressions, including more years of tornadoes and more county-level control variables.

We also investigate the role of tornado warnings on casualties. Specifically, we focus on whether a longer lead time reduces casualties, or whether instead there is an optimal lead time for a warning. Although responding to a tornado warning does not take long, for example, in contrast with evacuation for a hurricane, issuing the warning is just one part of the warning process. The warning must be disseminated to residents in harm's way via television, radio, tornado sirens, the Internet, or other channels, including phone calls from friends or relatives. Dissemination takes time, creating a need for longer lead times. We can determine from NWS tornado warning verification records whether each tornado was warned for or not. We have explored several ways to model warnings, including an indicator variable for whether a warning was issued for the tornado and the lead time on the warning in minutes (Simmons and Sutter 2008a). Here we focus on a set of dummy variables for lead times in the ranges of 1 to 5, 6 to 10, 11 to 15, 16 to 20, 21 to 30, and 31 or more minutes. The lead time is specifically the number of minutes between the time the warning was issued and the beginning of the tornado.[8] Creating intervals allows the marginal effect of lead time to vary in a possibly irregular manner.

Figure 6.4 presents the effect of lead time on fatalities and injuries. We again use an index to display the effect, with the index set equal to 100 for tornadoes with no warning or a warning lead time of zero minutes. An index value less than 100 indicates that lead time reduces casualties. Tornado warnings reduce injuries at all lead time intervals, with the largest reductions occurring in the 11 to 15 and 31+ minute intervals—42 percent and 44 percent, respectively. The reductions in injuries in the other lead time intervals range from 23 to 33 percent, and although the lead time variables are statistically significant, the differ-

Figure 6.4 Warning Lead Time and Casualties

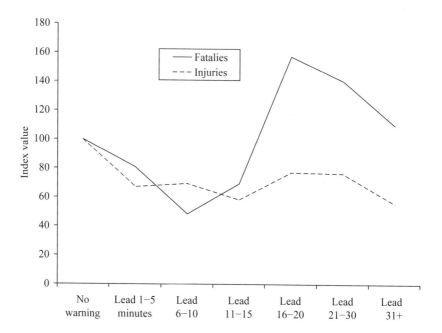

SOURCE: Authors' calculations from the NWS Storm Prediction Center's tornado archive.

ences between the intervals are not generally statistically significant. Thus warnings reduce injuries, but the marginal effect of lead time is essentially zero after 15 minutes.

The situation is different for fatalities. Lead times up to 15 minutes reduce fatalities by 19 percent, 51 percent, and 31 percent in the 1 to 5, 6 to 10, and 11 to 15 minute intervals, respectively. But lead times greater than 15 minutes increase fatalities relative to no warning, and by a sizable (and statistically significant) amount: 57 percent, 49 percent, and 11 percent for the 16 to 20, 21 to 30, and 31+ minute intervals, respectively. Some of these fatalities may occur because residents react to long lead times by taking actions that increase their risk relative to those taken when there is no warning. In addition, long lead times sometimes result when a warning is issued but not canceled and a tornado eventually occurs in the warning area; residents may not consider that such warnings convey the same degree of risk as those issued for an imminent tornado. As Simmons and Sutter (2008a) discuss, the increase in fatalities for long lead times reflects a handful of well-warned-of and particularly deadly tornadoes. A contributing factor is that powerful tornadoes tend to occur during large tornado outbreaks, and consequently are well warned of. We do not observe how many fatalities might result if the most powerful tornadoes occurred without warning. Furthermore, the warnings for some of these killer tornadoes may not have been disseminated to residents. For example, consider the 1987 Saragosa, Texas, tornado, which had a lead time of 22 minutes and resulted in 30 deaths. As Aguirre (1988) discusses, the fatalities occurred in an immigrant community where residents watched Spanish-language television networks that did not broadcast the warning, and thus they were effectively unwarned about the tornado.

While tornado warnings alert residents to danger, most warnings, because they are issued in advance of the tornado, turn out to be false alarms. The national false alarm ratio (FAR) was 0.744 in 2004, meaning that tornadoes did not occur in the warned county in three out of four cases. When warnings do not come to pass, the cry-wolf effect might apply: that is, residents might dismiss future warnings as false alarms, reducing the effectiveness of warnings that do precede tornadoes. A higher FAR reduces the value of the information contained in warnings, and should at some point reduce warning response. Yet a false alarm effect has been difficult to uncover: Barnes et al. (2007) find that "evidence for the cry-wolf effect in natural hazards research . . . has not been forthcoming" (p. 1142).

The extensive NWS tornado warning verification records allow a careful test of the effect of false alarms on tornado casualties, and by implication warning response. A complication arises because false alarms are nonevents, while tornadoes are events. It is not clear which tornado warnings, as regards both false alarms and verified warnings, should apply to constructing an FAR for different tornado events. If all warnings nationwide apply to all tornadoes, there will be no cross-sectional variation in FARs, and we would be forced to try to disentangle the effect of changes in the national FAR from a time trend. Warning performance, however, varies substantially across the nation as well as over time, and thus we use local, recent warnings to calculate an FAR in our analysis. Specifically, we use warnings issued in the state struck by a tornado over the previous 12 months to calculate an FAR that we use as a control variable in our regression analysis.[9]

We find strong evidence of a false alarm effect, consistent with economic models of the value of information. A higher state FAR significantly increases both fatalities and injuries. An increase of one standard deviation in the FAR (which is 0.117) increases expected fatalities by 10 percent and injuries by 9 percent. The national FAR declined after the NWS installed Doppler weather radars, so some of the reduction in casualties attributed above to Doppler radar (perhaps 10–20 percent of the 30–45 percent reduction) appears to have resulted from decreased false alarms. We have also calculated recent, local FARs using NWS Weather Forecast Office County Warning Areas and TV markets as defined by the A. C. Nielsen Company over one- and two-year intervals for robustness. We find a similar false alarm effect using these alternative FAR definitions (Simmons and Sutter 2009).

The dependence of casualties on time of day may constitute indirect evidence of the effectiveness of tornado warnings. Tornado warnings help reduce casualties only if people respond to them, and residents are probably less likely to receive warnings issued at night when they are asleep. Thus some portion of the lower fatalities and injuries for daytime tornadoes may be due to the lifesaving effects of tornado warnings.

The Demographics of Tornado Vulnerability

Economists have found that safety is generally a normal or luxury good: as people become wealthier and secure the necessities of life, they look to reduce risks of premature death. For natural hazards, Hurricane Katrina highlighted the converse of this proposition, the vulnerability of low-income households. Recent research has documented a negative relationship between income and natural hazards fatalities across countries (Anbarci, Escaleras, and Register 2005; Kahn 2005). Higher-income households could reduce tornado risk in several ways: by purchasing higher-quality homes (or not residing in manufactured homes), installing in-home tornado shelters, and purchasing NOAA weather radios or other emergency alert systems. Wealthier communities might be more likely to invest in tornado sirens and emergency management and emergency medical services.

Yet county-level income does not appear to reduce tornado fatalities or injuries. Our previous research (Simmons and Sutter 2005, 2008a) has shown that tornado paths through areas with higher median incomes have significantly greater fatalities and injuries, contrary to expectations. We include extra control variables in the regressions reported here, and the statistical significance of income is diminished, although an increase of one standard deviation in median income still increases expected fatalities and injuries by 8 to 9 percent. The income effect we found previously may be due to urbanization. Our previous and current regressions include population density, which as we would expect increases casualties since the number of persons in the path of a tornado affects the likelihood of casualties. Our regressions here also include the rural proportion of county population, as characterized by the Census Bureau; a larger rural population significantly reduces both fatalities and injuries. Urban areas have higher incomes than rural areas, and so the positive effect of income on casualties may be a residual consequence of a population effect.

Tornadoes seem to run counter to several other common elements of natural hazards vulnerability. The elderly are considered an at-risk population, and this vulnerability might be particularly acute for tornadoes, as the elderly may have difficulty hearing sirens or an approaching tornado and quickly moving to shelter without assistance. Yet a larger proportion of county residents over age 65 are associated with significantly reduced fatalities and injuries. Injuries also decrease with larger portions of residents under 18 and male residents. Poverty is normally associated with greater vulnerability, and here we have mixed evidence: an increased county poverty rate increases (although not significantly) expected fatalities and reduces expected injuries. But poverty likely affects the propensity of a household to live in manufactured housing, and this definitely increases vulnerability. Education is also related to vulnerability. A low level of education as indicated by the proportion of residents over age 25 who did not graduate from high school increases both fatalities and injuries. But the proportion of persons with a four-year college degree does not affect casualties. Long commuting times might also affect vulnerability to tornadoes, particularly since many tornadoes occur during the evening rush hour. We find some evidence of the vulnerability of commuters, as a higher proportion of residents with a commute over 30 minutes significantly increases fatalities but does not affect injuries.

HOW MIGHT TORNADO IMPACTS BE REDUCED?

Our analysis of tornado impacts can assist in evaluating alternatives for reducing impacts. Economics provides numerous examples of policies that fail to achieve their goal or even have unintended negative consequences. Several options exist for trying to reduce tornado impacts, and our analysis can help evaluate the comparative advantages and possible interactions between these alternatives. Based on our analysis we offer four insights on reducing tornado impacts. Note that the potential gain in reduced casualties from one measure falls when other measures are simultaneously employed. For example, the United States currently experiences about 60 tornado fatalities per year. A measure that reduces fatalities by 25 percent would currently save about 15 lives per year. If another measure first reduces fatalities to 40 per year, the 25 percent reduction in fatalities now saves 10 lives per year, and so the benefits of the measure fall by one-third. Thus our statements about potential casualty reductions are all based on recent casualties and assume no other measures are employed.

Tornado Warnings

As previously discussed, the value of time spent under warnings represents a significant portion of the societal cost of tornadoes. A recent NWS innovation will significantly reduce the amount of time spent under warnings. The NWS introduced Storm Based Warnings (SBWs) for tornadoes (and other types of severe weather) nationwide in October 2007. SBWs warn for a polygon area near the tornado circulation, not an entire county. In tests the new warnings reduced the area warned by 70 to 75 percent compared with county warnings, with no compromise of safety since residents actually at risk from the possible tornado are still warned (Looney 2006; Jacks and Ferree 2007). The new warnings will significantly benefit society, although the savings of time sheltering depends on how many people actually responded to county warnings. Assuming a 50 percent response rate to county warnings and a 70 percent reduction in warned area, SBWs will reduce the value of time spent sheltering by $1 billion per year (Sutter and Erickson, forthcoming). SBWs could help reduce tornado casualties as well, since more precise and hence valuable information in the new warnings should improve response. Counties are large relative to tornado damage paths: the area of the typical county struck by tornadoes is about 1,000 square miles, compared to a mean tornado damage area of 0.3 square miles.[10] Thus the old county warnings provided relatively little detail on the location of a possible tornado. By conveying a higher level of risk for the warned area, SBWs might make residents more likely to abandon a manufactured home, as the NWS recommends, and increase the value of NOAA weather radios and commercial emergency alert systems. The technology exists to convey even more precise information on the location of a tornado—for instance, through street-level storm tracking currently provided by some television stations.

Improved lead time for unwarned tornadoes can also reduce casualties. An optimal warning lead time reduces fatalities and injuries by 50 percent and 42 percent, respectively, relative to no warning. Between 2000 and 2004, 46 percent of tornadoes occurred with a warning lead time of five minutes or less. These tornadoes are underwarned for, in that our analysis shows that longer lead times should reduce casualties. Optimal warning for these tornadoes would reduce fatalities and injuries by an additional 21 percent and 15 percent, respectively. Given current warning technology, these tornadoes could not be warned for without increasing the FAR, and that would increase casualties. Improving lead time performance without increasing the FAR would require new technology or algorithms that shift the trade-off between detection and false alarms (see Brooks 2004 for a depiction of this trade-off).

On the other hand, we find no evidence that increasing lead times beyond 15 minutes would benefit society. In fact, longer lead times perversely result in more fatalities than a tornado without a warning. Although we think that this result may be anomalous, it does not follow that we would be likely to find a further reduction in fatalities beyond that observed in the 6 to 10 minute interval. And for injuries the marginal benefit of lead time beyond the 11 to 15 minute interval is essentially zero. This diminishing return probably occurs because residents can respond to a tornado warning—take cover in an interior room or storm shelter if available—quite quickly. Time is needed to disseminate a warning, but our results suggest that everyone who is likely to receive a warning has received it within 10 or 15 minutes. Thus our analysis of casualties leads us to expect that increased lead times beyond 15 minutes would not yield significant benefits to society.

Tornado Shelters: Rarely Cost-Effective

Engineers have designed above-ground safe rooms and below-ground shelters capable of protecting residents from even the strongest tornadoes. Below-ground shelters retail for $2,000 to $2,500, while safe rooms cost in excess of $5,000. The Federal Emergency Management Agency (FEMA) included tornado shelters in its National Mitigation Strategy in the 1990s and issued performance criteria for shelters (FEMA 1999). FEMA and the state of Oklahoma collaborated on the Oklahoma Saferoom Initiative to provide rebates to homeowners installing a shelter or safe room.

The evidence suggests that tornado shelters are not a cost-effective way to reduce permanent home casualties. Merrell, Simmons, and Sutter (2005) and Simmons and Sutter (2006) calculated the cost per life saved for shelters using historical casualties, predicted casualties from a regression model, and casualties per home struck by tornadoes. All three methods yield fairly consistent estimates for permanent homes; for instance, the cost per life saved in Oklahoma, at the heart of Tornado Alley, was over $50 million, which greatly exceeds market-revealed values of a statistical life (typically under $10 million). We illustrate the arithmetic with the historical fatality totals for Oklahoma, which experienced 263 tornado fatalities between 1950 and 2007, or 4.5 per year. In-home shelters can be expected to prevent only the 31 percent of fatalities that occur in permanent homes (see Figure 6.1). If all permanent home fatalities could be prevented, shelters would prevent 1.4 deaths per year.[11] The cost of equipping all of the more than one million single-family homes in the state with a shelter (at $2,000 per shelter) is over

$2 billion. The resulting cost per life saved in this calculation is $57 million. As another way of understanding this result, 55 percent of permanent home fatalities occur in F4 and F5 tornadoes. Violent tornadoes occur too infrequently even in Tornado Alley to justify economically such an expenditure, regardless of the potentially fatal consequences. Hardening targets is an ineffective way to reduce permanent home fatalities.

Reducing Manufactured Home Vulnerability

Reducing the vulnerability of manufactured homes is crucial to reducing tornado casualties. Although tornado shelters are unlikely to be cost-effective in permanent homes, the cost per life saved for mobile homes is less than $10 million in the most tornado-prone states. And the cost per life saved could be even lower with cost-sharing for shelters in manufactured home parks. Schmidlin, Hammer, and Knabe (2001) report that manufactured home parks do in fact offer community shelters as an amenity for residents. Simmons and Sutter (2007) find that lots in parks in Oklahoma with shelters rent at a 5 percent premium, which approximately covers the cost of a community shelter as estimated by FEMA (2000). Thus tornado shelters may help with the mobile home problem, but they are only part of the answer, and will be less effective for the majority of homes not located in a park.

Manufactured homes can also be made more wind-resistant. The Department of Housing and Urban Development in 1994 amended the HUD code for manufactured housing to include wind load requirements in areas subject to high winds. Although intended to reduce hurricane-related damage (to which end the rule has been effective; see Grosskopf 2005), the wind load provisions appear to reduce tornado risk as well. Simmons and Sutter (2008b) examined the aftermath of the February 2007 tornadoes in Lake County, Florida, which killed 21 persons, all in manufactured homes. A key factor in fatalities was whether the home was totally leveled, as characterized by county officials: 16 of the 17 fatalities for which home condition could be ascertained occurred in leveled homes. Manufactured homes built to the wind load provisions were 79 percent less likely to be leveled than homes built before the HUD code went into effect. No fatalities could be documented in the newer homes, and the reduction in the probability of a home being leveled implies that in time fatalities could be reduced by as much as 70 percent. Of course, whether these results extrapolate to other tornadoes (either stronger or weaker) is an open question, but improved construction may help mitigate the mobile home problem.

Tornadoes after Dark

Tornadoes are significantly more dangerous at night than during the day. Casualties could be reduced if the lethality of nighttime tornadoes could be brought in line with tornadoes during the day. Between 1986 and 2004, 177 and 116 fatalities and 2,871 and 2,217 injuries occurred in late evening (8 p.m.–midnight) and overnight (midnight–6 a.m.) tornadoes, respectively. If these tornadoes were only as dangerous as early afternoon tornadoes, 155 fatalities and 1,308 injuries would have been avoided. Overall this would reduce fatalities by 16 percent and injuries by 7 percent.

A strategy to reduce this vulnerability depends on exactly why nighttime tornadoes are so lethal, which is an area of ongoing research. Three alternative explanations seem plausible. First, the warning process might be less effective for nighttime tornadoes. That is, fewer people might receive these warnings because they happen to be asleep, as mentioned above. Second, and closely related, the response to nighttime warnings could differ. For instance, people might seek visual confirmation of a tornado before reacting, and the difficulty of seeing tornadoes at night might make people less likely to respond. Finally, the nighttime effect might be a consequence of the greater vulnerability of manufactured homes, since residents are more likely to be at home at night than during the day.[12] If the vulnerability to tornadoes after dark is due to less effective warnings, emergency alert systems or more refined warnings might reduce this vulnerability. If nighttime fatalities are an extension of the mobile home problem, the HUD wind load provisions or tornado shelters in mobile home parks might address the problem.

CONCLUSION

Our investigation has identified several aspects of the distribution of tornado casualties and the relative likelihood of casualties. A handful of powerful (F3 or stronger) tornadoes, often clustered on super tornado outbreak days, account for a large fraction of total casualties. But the distribution of fatalities or injuries by F-scale does not tell us in which category society could most easily reduce casualties. We have found that tornadoes that strike mobile homes or after dark or on weekends or during the fall or winter months produce more casualties. If casualties in these circumstances could be reduced to the comparable rate in permanent homes for weekday tornadoes during the spring season, the toll from tornadoes would be reduced considerably. But overall casualties are not currently the largest component of the societal cost of tornadoes. Because tornadoes have become less deadly over the years, property damage and the cost of responding to warnings now account for the bulk of their societal impact. The introduction of Storm Based Warnings by the NWS will reduce time spent under warnings by perhaps 70 percent.

Our quantitative, large data set analysis also reveals some promising directions for qualitative, survey, or case study analysis. Large data set statistical analysis excels at identifying patterns in vulnerability but does not necessarily allow us to pinpoint the cause of the vulnerability. A relatively small number of tornadoes account for many of the fatalities and injuries that drive our regression results; detailed case studies could help reveal whether special circumstances or details about the dissemination of warnings not readily captured by control variables contributed to the loss of life. Future qualitative research could help to address some of the casualty disparities. For instance, surveys could explore whether people respond differently to tornadoes at night or during the fall and winter months. Additional quantitative and qualitative research will be needed to reduce the societal impacts of tornadoes in a cost-effective manner.

Notes

We are grateful for continued financial support from NOAA's National Severe Storms Laboratory, the Institute for Catastrophic Loss Reduction, and the Natural Hazards Center at the University of Colorado.

1. Information on property damage, and on injuries and fatalities resulting from tornadoes in the following paragraphs, is from NOAA's National Weather Service Storm Prediction Center (SPC) Historical Severe Storm Database, http://www.spc .noaa.gov/wcm/index.html#data.
2. Brooks and Doswell (2001) present damage totals for past tornadoes adjusted for inflation, population growth, and changes in national wealth. The May 3, 1999, F5 tornado ranks eleventh in their adjusted damage calculations.
3. For a discussion of the concept of a statistical life and a survey of estimates from the market, see Viscusi, Vernon, and Harrington (2000).
4. National Oceanic and Atmospheric Administration (NOAA) Tornado Warning Verification Archive (StormDat), available from NOAA by permission.
5. The SPC archive can be accessed online at http://www.spc.noaa.gov/archive.
6. The Fujita scale rates tornado damage from F0 (weakest) to F5 (strongest). An F0 is a minimal tornado that causes light damage; an F5 tornado causes "incredible" damage, including well-built homes swept off their foundations and cars thrown more than 100 meters. A description of the Fujita scale and the Enhanced Fujita scale can be found at http://www.spc.noaa.gov/faq/tornado/f-scale.html.
7. National Oceanic and Atmospheric Administration (NOAA) Tornado Fatality Locations, available from NOAA by permission.
8. By convention, the NWS counts a case where a tornado warning is issued after the tornado is on the ground as a warned tornado with a lead time of zero. We had previously separated out zero lead time tornadoes as an extra category, but the effect of a zero lead time warning was very close to (and statistically indistinguishable from) no warning.
9. These regressions omit tornadoes for which no warnings were issued in the state in the prior 12 months, since the FAR in these instances is undefined.
10. Authors' calculation using NOAA's National Weather Service Storm Prediction Center (SPC) Historical Severe Storm Database, http://www.spc.noaa.gov/wcm/ index.html#data.
11. And even then shelters would prevent all in-home fatalities only if residents always take shelter before the tornado hits.
12. Note that residual mobile home vulnerability could also explain the greater lethality of tornadoes on weekends.

Appendix 6A

The impacts on tornado casualties discussed throughout this chapter are from a regression analysis of casualties. This appendix describes the details of the regression models. Fatalities and injuries take on nonnegative integer values; that is, the number of persons killed in a tornado can equal 0, 1, 2, or more, with a large number of zero observations. Ordinary least squares regression fails to take into account the truncation of casualties at zero, and thus instead a Poisson regression model is applied to this count data. The Poisson model (Greene 2000, pp. 880–886) assumes that the dependent variable y_i is drawn from a Poisson distribution with parameter λ_i, or

$$\text{Prob}(Y_i = y_i) = e^{-\lambda i} \times \lambda_i^{yi}/y_i!, \, y_i = 0, 1, 2, \ldots$$

The parameter λ_i of the distribution is assumed to be a log-linear function of the independent variables x_i, or $ln(\lambda_i) = \beta' \times x_i$. The Poisson regression model assumes equivalence of the conditional mean of y_i and its variance; violation of this condition is known as overdispersion. The negative binomial regression model (Greene 2000, pp. 886–888), a generalization of the Poisson model, is recommended when the data exhibit overdispersion. Diagnostic tests consistently indicate that injuries but not fatalities are overdispersed. Consequently we estimate fatalities with Poisson models and injuries with negative binomial models.

Our models include three categories of variables, describing characteristics of the tornado, the tornado path, and NWS efforts to reduce casualties. The models also include, but we do not report, year dummy variables. The year variables control for nationwide changes over time, such as the advent of the Internet as a channel to communicate warnings, and any possible year-to-year variation in warning response. The tornado characteristic variables are as described in the text, and model the rating of the tornado on the F-scale of tornado damage, the time of day, month, and whether the tornado occurred on a weekend. We also include the length of the damage path in miles.

The storm path variables control for the economic and demographic characteristics of the area struck by the tornado. The variable labels in Table 6A.1 are self-descriptive. The variables are constructed using census data for the counties reported as in the storm path. For a tornado that struck more than one county, the tornado path variables average the observations for each county in the storm path. The path variables for a specific year are based on linear interpolation from the decennial censuses. For tornadoes after 2000, population density is calculated using the census annual population estimates, while other variables use linear interpolation with county data from the 2006 American Community Survey when available. Mobile homes as a proportion of housing units by county was not reported in census publications prior to 1990, so for 1986–1989 tornadoes, the values from the 1990 census are used. We also include an interaction term between path length and population density, because a long-track tornado through a highly populated area might affect casualties differently from an increase in either of these variables separately.

The NWS variables are a dummy variable for tornadoes that occurred after installation of Doppler radar and tornado warning. The Doppler variable equals 1 if the tornado occurred on or after the date on which Doppler radar was installed in the NWS Weather Forecast Office with warning responsibility for the first tornado in the storm's path. Since warnings are issued by county, a tornado that strikes several counties may yield several valid warnings. We apply the warning for the first county in the storm path. The tornado warning variables are dummy variables that indicate whether the lead time in minutes for the warning (if any) for the first county in the storm path was in this interval. The False Alarm Ratio (FAR) variable is the proportion of warnings issued in the state struck by the tornado in the prior 12 months that were false alarms (i.e., that did not verify, as defined by the NWS). Table 6A.1 reports one specification of the casualties regressions with the Doppler radar variable but no warning variables, and one specification with the warning variables but not the Doppler variable. The Doppler radar specifications test for an impact of radar installation on casualties, which could be due to better warning for tornadoes or improved warning response.

Table 6A.1 reports the raw regression coefficients and standard errors. To interpret the coefficients as discussed in the text, the antilog of the coefficient must be taken. Thus to calculate the marginal effect of a dummy variable with coefficient β_k from the table, the percentage change in expected casualties is $100 \times (\exp[\beta_k] - 1)$. The percentage change in expected casualties due to a one standard deviation increase in variable k, σ_k, in variable k is $100 \times (\exp[\beta_k \times \sigma_k] - 1)$. Note that for a set of mutually exclusive categories (F-scale categories, day parts, months of the year), one of the dummy variable categories must be omitted for the model to be estimated. The impact of the included variables is then measured relative to that of a tornado in the excluded category: overnight for day parts, July for month, and F0 for F-scale. Table 6A.1 also indicates the statistical significance of each of the coefficient estimates at two different levels, 10 percent and 1 percent, in a two-tailed test of the null hypothesis that the coefficient is zero.

Table 6A.1 Regression Analysis of Tornado Fatalities and Injuries

	Fatalities (Doppler, no warning)[a]	Fatalities (warning, no Doppler)[a]	Injuries (Doppler, no warning)[a]	Injuries (warning, no Doppler)[a]
Doppler		−0.354* (0.240)		−0.581*** (0.174)
FAR	0.784* (0.353)		0.702*** (0.262)	
Lead 1–5 min.	−0.223* (0.134)		−0.396*** (0.123)	
Lead 6–10 min.	−0.727*** (0.145)		−0.363*** (0.119)	
Lead 11–15 min.	−0.369* (0.160)		−0.538*** (0.127)	
Lead 16–20 min.	0.446*** (0.132)		−0.257* (0.137)	
Lead 21–30 min.	0.336*** (0.114)		−0.265* (0.119)	
Lead 31+ min.	0.0879 (0.134)		−0.582*** (0.124)	
Morning	−0.808*** (0.174)	−0.903*** (0.174)	−0.0882 (0.144)	−0.0536 (0.140)
Early afternoon	−0.846*** (0.132)	−0.891*** (0.131)	−0.359*** (0.126)	−0.436*** (0.123)
Early evening	−0.664*** (0.124)	−0.592*** (0.121)	−0.323*** (0.121)	−0.386*** (0.118)
Late evening	−0.154 (0.133)	−0.147 (0.131)	−0.0816 (0.137)	−0.161 (0.134)
Weekend	0.334*** (0.0847)	0.313*** (0.0836)	0.0793 (0.0704)	0.0853 (0.0688)
January	1.45*** (0.391)	1.03*** (0.352)	0.521*** (0.192)	0.536*** (0.186)
February	2.70*** (0.366)	2.19*** (0.323)	0.332 (0.210)	0.372* (0.201)
March	1.89*** (0.353)	1.42*** (0.311)	0.305* (0.161)	0.236 (0.154)
April	1.49*** (0.348)	0.993*** (0.307)	0.0702 (0.140)	0.0554 (0.136)

(continued)

Table 6A.1   (continued)

	Fatalities (Doppler, no warning)[a]	Fatalities (warning, no Doppler)[a]	Injuries (Doppler, no warning)[a]	Injuries (warning, no Doppler)[a]
May	1.44***	1.12***	−0.408***	−0.473***
	(0.341)	(0.298)	(0.129)	(0.125)
June	0.944*	0.506	−0.187	−0.226*
	(0.375)	(0.336)	(0.132)	(0.129)
August	2.48***	2.07***	−0.161	−0.0645
	(0.366)	(0.323)	(0.169)	(0.162)
September	1.68***	1.05***	−0.0892	−0.109
	(0.420)	(0.387)	(0.172)	(0.168)
October	2.16***	1.60***	0.0360	0.0064
	(0.393)	(0.357)	(0.173)	(0.169)
November	2.10***	1.70***	0.269*	0.317*
	(0.354)	(0.313)	(0.153)	(0.150)
December	2.20***	1.74***	0.0023	0.0795
	(0.392)	(0.355)	(0.241)	(0.234)
Density	0.000251	0.0000	0.0029***	0.0003***
	(0.000995)	(0.0001)	(0.0007)	(0.0001)
Mobiles	3.67***	4.04***	2.79***	3.07***
	(0.660)	(0.654)	(0.529)	(0.526)
Income	0.00865	0.0118	0.0077	0.0159*
	(0.00915)	(0.0091)	(0.0083)	(0.0081)
Rural	−1.40***	−1.57***	−0.598***	−0.616***
	(0.212)	(0.218)	(0.155)	(0.153)
Nonwhite	−0.898*	−1.03***	0.657*	0.593*
	(0.367)	(0.363)	(0.313)	(0.306)
Male	2.42	2.17	−6.54***	−6.59***
	(2.47)	(2.40)	(2.02)	(1.99)
Under 18	1.53	1.53	−5.19***	−5.83***
	(1.81)	(1.74)	(1.37)	(1.34)
Over 65	−3.94*	−5.56***	−5.54***	−5.59***
	(1.69)	(1.65)	(1.11)	(1.08)
Commute 30+ min.	2.19***	2.30***	0.361	0.0932
	(0.413)	(0.458)	(0.351)	(0.381)
No high school	1.81*	1.45*	3.07***	3.63***
	(0.791)	(0.786)	(0.662)	(0.646)

Table 6A.1 (continued)

	Fatalities (Doppler, no warning)[a]	Fatalities (warning, no Doppler)[a]	Injuries (Doppler, no warning)[a]	Injuries (warning, no Doppler)[a]
College	−0.244 (0.840)	−1.41* (0.836)	−0.0540 (0.694)	−0.0097 (0.683)
Poverty rate	1.48 (1.16)	1.75 (1.27)	−2.43* (1.03)	−2.06* (1.01)
Length	0.1002*** (0.0214)	0.0008*** (0.0002)	0.347*** (0.0592)	0.0032*** (0.0006)
Length × density	0.0006 (0.0008)	0.0000 (0.0000)	0.0072*** (0.0020)	0.0001*** (0.0000)
F1	2.73*** (0.374)	−10.5*** (1.71)	2.40*** (0.0810)	0.672 (1.30)
F2	4.65*** (0.365)		4.17*** (0.101)	
F3	6.30*** (0.364)		5.18*** (0.154)	
F4	7.88*** (0.368)		6.54*** (0.255)	
F5	10.19*** (0.387)		7.50*** (0.867)	
Intercept	−10.5*** (1.83)		0.282 (1.35)	
# observations	20,605		20,605	
Log likelihood	−1,797		−9,400	

NOTE: Fatality estimates use Poisson regression models and injuries use negative binomial models with standard errors in parentheses. *significant at the 0.10 level (two-tailed test); ***significant at the 0.01 level (two-tailed test).
[a] See Appendix 6A for the distinction in the two calculations of fatalities and injuries.
SOURCE: Authors' calculations from SPC, NWS, and U.S. census data.

References

Aguirre, Begnino E. 1988. "The Lack of Warnings before the Saragosa Torna-do." *International Journal of Mass Emergencies and Disaster* 6(1): 65–74.
American Meteorological Society. 1997. "Policy Statement: Mobile Homes and Severe Windstorms." *Bulletin of the American Meteorological Society* 78(5): 850–851.
Anbarci, Nejat, Monica Escaleras, and Charles A. Register. 2005. "Earthquake Fatalities: The Interaction of Nature and Political Economy." *Journal of Public Economics* 89(9–10): 1907–1933.
Ashley, Walker S., A.J. Knmenec, and Richard Schwantes. 2008. "Vulnerabil-ity Due to Nocturnal Tornadoes." *Weather and Forecasting* 23(5): 795–807.
Barnes, Lindsay R., Eve C. Gruntfest, Mary H. Hayden, David M. Schultz, and Charles Benight. 2007. "False Alarms and Close Calls: A Conceptual Model of Warning Accuracy." *Weather and Forecasting* 22(5): 1140–1147.
Brooks, Harold E. 2004. "Tornado-Warning Performance in the Past and Fu-ture: A Perspective from Signal Detection Theory." *Bulletin of the American Meteorological Society* 85(6): 837–843.
Brooks, Harold E., and Charles A. Doswell III. 2001. "Normalized Damage from Major Tornadoes in the United States: 1890–1999." *Weather and Forecasting* 16(1): 168–176.
———. 2002. "Deaths in the 3 May 1999 Oklahoma City Tornado from a His-torical Perspective." *Weather and Forecasting* 17(3): 354–361.
Brown, Sheryll, Pam Archer, Elizabeth Kruger, and Sue Mallonee. 2002. "Tor-nado-Related Deaths and Injuries in Oklahoma Due to the 3 May 1999 Tor-nadoes." *Weather and Forecasting* 17(3): 343–353.
Bureau of Labor Statistics (BLS). 2007. *Establishment Data, Historical Hours and Earnings: B-2. Average Hours and Earnings of Production and Nonsupervisory Employees on Private Nonfarm Payrolls by Major In-dustry Sector, 1964 to Date.* Washington, DC: Bureau of Labor Statistics. ftp://146.142.4.23/pub/suppl/empsit.ceseeb2.txt (accessed December 9, 2009).
Camerer, Colin F., and Howard Kunreuther. 1989. "Decision Processes for Low Probability Events: Policy Implications." *Journal of Policy Analysis and Management* 8(4): 565–592.
Carter, A.O., M.E. Millson, and D.E. Allen. 1989. "Epidemiologic Study of Deaths and Injuries Due to Tornadoes." *American Journal of Epidemiology* 130(6): 1209–1218.
Doswell, Charles A. III, Alan R. Moller, and Harold E. Brooks. 1999. "Storm Spotting and Public Awareness since the First Tornado Forecasts of 1948." *Weather and Forecasting* 14(4): 544–557.

Environmental Protection Agency (EPA). 1997. *The Benefits and Costs of the Clean Air Act, 1970 to 1990*. http://www.epa.gov/airprogm/oar/sect812/index.html (accessed December 9, 2009).

Federal Emergency Management Agency (FEMA). 1999. *Taking Shelter from the Storm: Building a Safe Room Inside Your House*. 2d ed. Publication 320. Washington, DC: Federal Emergency Management Agency.

———. 2000. *Design and Construction Guidance for Community Shelters*. Publication 361. Washington, DC: Federal Emergency Management Agency.

Golden, Joseph H., and Christopher R. Adams. 2000. "The Tornado Problem: Forecast, Warning, and Response." *Natural Hazards Review* 1(2): 107–118.

Golden, Joseph H., and John T. Snow. 1991. "Mitigation against Extreme Windstorms." *Reviews of Geophysics* 29(4): 477–504.

Greene, William H. 2000. *Econometric Analysis*. 4th ed. Upper Saddle River, NJ: Prentice Hall.

Grosskopf, Kevin R. 2005. "Assessing the Effectiveness of Mitigation: A Case Study of Manufactured Housing and the 2004 Hurricane Season." *Journal of Emergency Management* 3(5): 27–32.

Jacks, Eli, and John Ferree. 2007. "Socio-Economic Impacts of Storm-Based Warnings." Paper presented at the 2d Symposium in Policy and Socio-Economic Impacts, held in San Antonio, TX, January 15–18.

Kahn, Matthew E. 2005. "The Death Toll from Natural Disasters: The Role of Income, Geography, and Institutions." *Review of Economics and Statistics* 87(2): 271–284.

Looney, Michael. 2006. "Polygon Warnings: The Sharp Focus on Service." Presentation to the Central Regional Managers' Conference, held in Kansas City, MO, March 7.

Martinez, Maribel, and Bradley Ewing. 2008. "A Look at the Economic Impact of Tornado Induced Damage in Tulia, Texas." Paper presented at the 2008 Hazards and Disaster Researchers Meeting, held in Broomfield, CO, July 15–16.

McClelland, Gary H., William D. Schulze, and Don L. Coursey. 1993. "Insurance for Low-Probability Hazards: A Bimodal Response to Unlikely Events." *Journal of Risk and Uncertainty* 7(1): 95–116.

Merrell, David, Kevin M. Simmons, and Daniel Sutter. 2005. "The Determinants of Tornado Casualties and the Benefits of Tornado Shelters." *Land Economics* 81(1): 87–99.

Meyer, Robert J. 2006. "Why We Under-Prepare for Hazards." In *On Risk and Disaster: Lessons from Hurricane Katrina*, Ronald J. Daniels, Donald F. Kettl, and Howard Kunreuther, eds. Philadelphia: University of Pennsylvania Press, pp. 153–173.

Schmidlin, Thomas W., Barbara Hammer, and Jodanna Knabe. 2001. "Tornado

Shelters in Mobile Home Parks in the United States." *Journal of the American Society of Professional Emergency Planners* 8: 1–15.

Simmons, Kevin M., and Daniel Sutter. 2005. "WSR-88D Radar, Tornado Warnings, and Tornado Casualties." *Weather and Forecasting* 20(3): 301–310.

———. 2006. "Direct Estimation of the Cost Effectiveness of Tornado Shelters." *Risk Analysis* 26(4): 345–354.

———. 2007. "Tornado Shelters and the Manufactured Home Parks Market." *Natural Hazards* 43(3): 365–378.

———. 2008a. "Tornado Warnings, Lead Times, and Tornado Casualties: An Empirical Investigation." *Weather and Forecasting* 23(3): 246–258.

———. 2008b. "Manufactured Home Building Regulations and the February 2, 2007, Florida Tornadoes." *Natural Hazards* 46(3): 415–425.

———. 2009. "False Alarms, Tornado Warnings, and Tornado Casualties." *Weather, Climate and Society* 1(1): 39–53.

Sutter, Daniel, and Somer Erickson. Forthcoming. "The Value of Tornado Warnings and Improvements in Warnings." *Weather, Climate and Society.*

U.S. Census Bureau. 2000. *Historical Census of Housing Tables—Units in Structure.* http://www.census.gov/hhes/www/housing/census/historic/units .html (accessed December 9, 2009).

Viscusi, W. Kip, John M. Vernon, and Joseph E. Harrington Jr. 2000. *Economics of Regulation and Antitrust.* 3d ed. Cambridge, MA: MIT Press.

The Authors

Peter J. Boettke is BB&T Professor for the Study of Capitalism at the Mercatus Center at George Mason University, and University Professor of Economics at George Mason University.

Hal Cochane is a fellow at Colorado State University's Cooperative Institute for Research in the Atmosphere (CIRA). Before that he was professor of economics at CSU and a senior research scientist at CIRA.

William Kern is professor and chair of the Department of Economics at Western Michigan University. His research interests include the history of economic thought, sports economics, and comparative economic systems. He is the editor of two previous volumes in this series: *From Socialism to Market Economy* (1992) and *The Economics of Sports* (2000).

Howard C. Kunreuther is the Cecilia Yen Koo Professor of Decision Sciences and Public Policy of the Wharton School, University of Pennsylvania, and co-director of the Wharton Risk Management and Decision Processes Center.

Erwann O. Michel-Kerjan is the managing director of the Wharton Risk Management and Decision Processes Center and teaches value creation in the Wharton MBA program.

Kevin M. Simmons holds the Corrigan Chair of Economics at Austin College. He holds a PhD in economics from Texas Tech University, where he developed a research interest in the economics of natural hazards.

Daniel J. Smith is a Mercatus PhD Fellow and third-year PhD student in economics at George Mason University. He is conducting research in the fields of political economy and law and economics.

Daniel Sutter received his PhD from George Mason University and is an associate professor of economics at the University of Texas–Pan American. His research interests include the societal impacts of extreme weather and natural disasters, public choice and regulation, the news media, and the markets for ideas and academics.

Anthony M. Yezer is professor of economics and director of the Center for Economic Research at George Washington University. His primary areas of teaching and research are regional and urban economics.

Index

The italic letters *f*, *n*, and *t* following a page number indicate that the subject information of the heading is within a figure, note, or table, respectively, on that page. Double italics indicate multiple but consecutive elements.

Alabama hurricanes, losses in, 19*t*

Alaska earthquakes, economics after, 44, 66

American Community Survey, annual census estimates from, 126

Atlanta, Georgia, as Katrina-survivor destination, 93

Bombing raids, recovery from, 66

Broadcast media, tornado warnings on, 112, 115–116, 119

Building codes
city government enforcement of, 26
mitigation measures and, 22, 35*n*5
private sector thwarted by, in disaster recovery, 5, 93

Burton, Ian, as disaster economics pioneer, 66

California earthquakes
hazard awareness in, 25–26, 42, 60*nn*4–5
insured losses in, 13, 16*t*
property value changes after, 56

Canadian tornadoes, hospitalizations from, 105

Carbon dioxide emissions, 4, 70–71

Caribbean Basin hurricanes, losses in, 10, 16*t*–17*t*

Casualties from disasters, 10, 16*t*–17*t*, 72
fatalities and injuries included in, 105, 125–126, 127*t*–129*t*
See also under specific kinds of disasters, e.g., Earthquakes; Floods; Tornadoes

Catastrophes. *See* Disasters

CGEs. *See* Computable general equilibrium models

Charitable organizations, high-risk areas and, 88, 90–91, 99

Charley (hurricane), 13, 16*t*, 19*t*

Chicago, Illinois, commuting congestion in, 50, 61*n*16

Child care centers, adult-to-child ratio in, 93

Chinese earthquakes, Sichuan casualties in, 10

Churches, reestablishing community services by, 88, 98, 99

City governments
coastal planning authority of, 49
land development policies by, 5, 26
(*see also under specific cities, e.g.,* New Orleans, Louisiana)
licensing and permits by, 92–93

Clean Air Act, 105

Climate debates. *See* Global climate change

Coastal Barrier Resources Act, 49

Coastal regions, 20
climate change debate and, 69–71
definition, 35*n*5
population concentration in, 10, 15, 18, 96, 97*t*, 100*n*2

Coastal Zone Management Act, 49

Collisions, as man-made disasters, 14*f*

Colombian hurricanes, losses in, 17*t*

Colorado State University, supply shock algorithm developed by, 76, 77*f*, 78, 80, 80*f*

Computable general equilibrium models (CGEs), economic response to shocks and, 74–75, 76, 78, 82

Connecticut hurricanes, losses in, 19*t*

Corps of Engineers. *See* U.S. Army Corps of Engineers

Japanese natural disasters, 16*t*, 17*t*, 56
Jeanne (hurricane), 13, 17*t*

Kansas, tornadoes and, 103
Kansas City, Missouri, commuting
    congestion in, 50, 61*n*15
Kates, Robert, as disaster economics
    pioneer, 66–67
Katrina (hurricane). *See* Hurricane
    Katrina
Kunreuther, Howard C., as disaster
    economics pioneer, 66, 71

Land development
    beach property damages from storms,
        53–56, 61*nn*20–22
    disaster expectations and mitigation
        upon, 49–51, 58–59, 61*nn*14–17
    disaster-prone areas and, 3–4, 5, 18,
        26, 33, 91
    market values and, 4, 15, 45, 62*n*26
Lave, Lester, retrospective work of, 67
Long-term insurance, 2–3, 26–32
Louisiana
    cities in
        (*see* New Orleans, Louisiana)
    corruption in, 89, 90, 93
    hurricane losses in, 10, 19*t*
        (*see also* Hurricane Katrina)
    insurance regulation in, as high-risk
        state, 91–92

Maass, Arthur, as disaster economics
    pioneer, 66–67
Man-made disasters
    anthropogenic carbon dioxide and,
        70–71
    in new era of catastrophes, 13–14, 14*f*
    recovery from, 65–66
    See also specific kinds, e.g., Terrorism
Manufactured homes
    construction regulations for, 7, 121–
        122
    tornado fatalities in, 108–109, 109*f*,
        124*n*12

Mary Queen of Vietnam Catholic
    Church, New Orleans,
    reestablishing community services
    by, 98, 99
Massachusetts hurricanes, losses in, 19*t*
Mill, John Stuart, quoted, 65, 87, 92
Mining accidents, as man-made disasters,
    14*f*
Mississippi hurricanes, losses in, 10, 19*t*
Missouri, urban commuting congestion
    in, 50, 61*n*15
Mobile homes. *See* Manufactured homes
Moral hazard
    in land development, 49–51, 61*nn*14–
        17
    protection from full cost of choices
        as, 91
    as Samaritan's dilemma, 49, 58,
        61*n*14
Myanmarian cyclones, casualties in, 10

National Flood Insurance Program
    (NFIP)
    assistance from, 49, 57, 62*n*25
    beachfront properties in, 54–56
    as opportunity to create long-term
        insurance markets, 2, 30–32, 34
    participation in, 31, 51, 61*n*18
National Oceanic and Atmospheric
    Administration (NOAA)
    storm data from, 107*t*, 124*n*1,
        124*nn*4–5, 124*n*7
    See also agencies of, e.g., National
        Weather Service (NWS)
National Weather Service (NWS)
    Doppler radar installations by, 112–
        113, 116
    tornado warning systems of, 6, 113–
        116, 114*f*, 124*n*8, 125, 126,
        127*t*–129*t*
Natural disaster syndrome, human
    behavior challenges and, 24–26,
    33, 61*n*19, 104
Natural disasters, 44
    human deaths by, 10, 103, 105, 106–
        107, 121

About the Institute

The W.E. Upjohn Institute for Employment Research is a nonprofit research organization devoted to finding and promoting solutions to employment-related problems at the national, state, and local levels. It is an activity of the W.E. Upjohn Unemployment Trustee Corporation, which was established in 1932 to administer a fund set aside by Dr. W.E. Upjohn, founder of The Upjohn Company, to seek ways to counteract the loss of employment income during economic downturns.

The Institute is funded largely by income from the W.E. Upjohn Unemployment Trust, supplemented by outside grants, contracts, and sales of publications. Activities of the Institute comprise the following elements: 1) a research program conducted by a resident staff of professional social scientists; 2) a competitive grant program, which expands and complements the internal research program by providing financial support to researchers outside the Institute; 3) a publications program, which provides the major vehicle for disseminating the research of staff and grantees, as well as other selected works in the field; and 4) an Employment Management Services division, which manages most of the publicly funded employment and training programs in the local area.

The broad objectives of the Institute's research, grant, and publication programs are to 1) promote scholarship and experimentation on issues of public and private employment and unemployment policy, and 2) make knowledge and scholarship relevant and useful to policymakers in their pursuit of solutions to employment and unemployment problems.

Current areas of concentration for these programs include causes, consequences, and measures to alleviate unemployment; social insurance and income maintenance programs; compensation; workforce quality; work arrangements; family labor issues; labor-management relations; and regional economic development and local labor markets.